Purpose - Driven Enterprise

Finding Your Purpose + Making It Your Paycheck

KENDRA Y. HILL

4

Dedication

To the girls who be "draped up, dripped out
- know what I'm talmbout?"

Oh, and to The Milli Club. Purr.

Contents

Preface

Purpose is by far the most elusive thing that exists on this planet. If I had a dollar for every time someone emailed or DM'd me about finding their purpose, I'd be richer than I've ever been. "What's my purpose? How can I find my purpose? Why won't God show me what I was made for?" It's like nobody knows what the heck is going on.

Through a really intense journey, I found my purpose in the comments section of a YouTube video on my own channel (chile, maybe I'll start posting again one day). I knew I had a pretty good idea about what my purpose was, but I had never been able to easily articulate it. Ultimately, the video about making your purpose your paycheck is how I solidified my own. After posting the video to my channel, I went through my normal routine - sharing to social, adding a post to my community tab, and pinning a comment to the top of the comments section. I wrote:

> "Hey hey! Do you know what your God-given purpose is? If so, share it down below! Mine is in the comments."

Followed by:

> "My purpose is to help motivate and inspire others to align themselves with God's plan for their lives."

I remember typing it and being shook by that statement. The very thing I had been searching for my entire life just showed up like an unannounced visitor that I needed to host in my home for the rest of my life. I cried for a very long time that day partially because the typing of my own fingers scared me. But I cried mostly because I finally felt whole, mature, and complete. I felt perfected.

That's what this book is all about. I want you to walk away from this experience (and yes, it will be an experience) knowing that God has a plan for your life and that it's not as spooky and mysterious as it may seem. I've read a lot of books about purpose, most of which either overcomplicate or oversimplify the topic in the hopes of making people buy more books, classes, and courses to make their teaching complete. I'm not doing that. I'm literally sitting on a horse farm nestled in the foothills of the Blue Ridge Mountains (near Dahlonega, GA) pouring out *my* life and the word of God concerning yours. If you've been spinning your wheels trying to get an answer, know that this time will be different.

HOW TO USE THIS BOOK

I designed this book to be part entertainment (my stories), part education (God's teachings), and part execution (your work). Purpose is not going to just jump off of these pages and find you. This isn't some type of osmosis or a magic trick. You will need to do the exercises as they come and fully commit to doing the work.

I know that the phrase "doing the work" is often used and not explained, so let me help you: you will need to face yourself internally and externally. You'll be pushed to face your demons. You'll have to tap into some of that old trauma and heal. You'll find yourself working and crying and feeling even more lost than when you started. When you get to *that* point, you've made it. Let yourself follow the instructions and the leading of the Holy Spirit to get you where you need to be.

Also, don't skip around. If you're anything like me, I try to circumvent the author of every book by figuring out the quickest way to get to the results. It won't work in this instance. You will need to go step-by-step and section-by-section to get everything you need. So resist the urge to be rebellious.

I initially went into this process planning to make a regular novel-sized book with long chapters and God quickly snatched that idea from me. The book is broken into bite-sized chapters, allowing you to consume and digest a lot of intense content in small doses. Trust me, you'll be glad that each chapter is only a few pages long.

THE EXPECTED END

Ultimately, my goal is to bring you to the peaceful pastures of purpose. I want you to walk away from this book (the first time, because you'll need it at different points of your life) with clarity and a plan to pursue the life that God has for you. You will feel refreshed, seen, heard, and recognized. And eventually, you will be able to fully tap into your best life by profiting from your purpose. That's it. That's all.

Let's pray:

> Lord, as we journey to purpose, I pray that You would open our eyes. That You would open our ears. That You would open our spirits to be receptive to whatever it is You have for us. If we're lost and we need direction, God we trust that this time is for that. Lord, if we feel confused about our business then help us use this time to pivot. I pray that You show us what's next and that You prepare us for the new levels and dimensions You're taking us to. Lord, do Your work in us. Help us tap into who You created us to be. In Jesus' name, Amen.

If at any point you want to ask me a question or interact with me, feel free to tag me on Instagram or Twitter (@iamkendrayhill) and use the hashtag #PurposeDrivenEnterprise. I'm more than happy to answer any questions or elaborate on anything I share here with you. My life is quite literally an open book.

INTRODUCTION: To the Windowwwwww, To the Wall

I've always struggled with purpose. I guess I just expected it to fall out of the sky and bop me in the head. There was always this idea that it would be some special moment - I don't know if I was hoping for fireworks or an angelic visitation, but it didn't happen like that. I discovered my purpose by unceremoniously commenting on my own YouTube video (did you read the preface or nah?).

Let me back up though as I don't want to oversimplify my discovery. The journey really started a longgggggg time ago, around 2013 when I was running an escort service in Washington DC. My former friend LaToya had moved to DC from Dallas to pursue her music career. She wanted me to manage her as I had been working in the entertainment industry for about 7 years already and I was well-connected.

One morning, we were sitting on my front porch talking and in typical LaToya fashion, she was lethargically smoking her blunt and whining. She was the type of person who had to wake and bake or she couldn't function. She turned to me with a sly expression. "I need to start making some real money," she said. I nodded in agreement. LaToya had only been there for 2 months and she was already eating me out of house and home with her munchies. After a few minutes of silence, she nonchalantly said, "I need to start hoeing again." While I knew a lot about LaToya (we had been friends since 4th grade), I had no idea that she had been a prostitute. I'm sure my facial response was meme-worthy. As I took the time to process the fact that my childhood friend had been having sex for money, LaToya went into her history as an escort in Oakcliff (South Dallas). Over the next hour or so, she convinced me to start an escort service with her where I would run the business aspect and she would teach the girls how to perform their duties.

I won't bore you with the details of the following months, but let me tell you, even then, purpose was chasing me down. At our peak, we had about 15 girls who were working with us, escorting the best (and the worst) men that the nation's capital had to offer. Though I had a beautiful 4 bedroom home in northwest DC, I spent most of my time at the Sheraton in Silver Spring, Maryland with LaToya and the girls. Literally, day and night, sitting in a hotel room with 2 beds and anywhere from 7-12 girls waiting to get booked for work. You could call me a madame (because I was), but most of those girls called me a mentor.

As soon as a new girl would start, I would find some one-on-one time to talk to them about their goals and dreams. Casually playing "Black Magic

Woman" by Carlos Santana on Guitar Hero, I would ask each girl what they wanted to be when they got out or what their childhood was like. A licensed minister since 2004, I had lots of experience dealing with lost souls - I just couldn't see that I needed a GPS too. "I want to be a nurse practitioner," Diona told me while sipping some syrup. Known as Erykah aka Chocolate Thunder, she was one of the busiest girls in the company. "So why are you here?" I asked. "Somebody gotta pay for school, right?" she replied while pulling on the blunt before passing it back to LaToya.

These interactions went on for months. I'd meet a new girl, interview her for the job and then interview her for her destiny. There were countless conversations about developing strategies to get out of escorting and moving into their purpose. I could feel God pulling on me to leave the escorting business alone, but I also loved making money. I kept having this reoccurring dream where I would see myself homeless and alone then God would show me living in a mansion with my own family. I'd wake up in a cold sweat and literally hear God say, "Release and trust Me." I just couldn't let it go, Elsa. I too was frozen. At our peak, we were making about $10,000 a week and there was no way I was giving up that kind of money. I was stuck in a cycle that was sick and dark with no way out.

I was in too deep.

Until one Monday morning. I was driving on the beltway to collect some money from one of the girls. This was my usual routine. I would stay up all night long and wait until about 5:00 am to meet up with two of my head girls to collect the money from the night before. I don't know if radio still works this way, but back then, the hip hop and RnB stations would play gospel music for about 30 minutes before The Tom Joyner Morning Show or Rickey Smiley. As I'm taking exit 31 to downtown Silver Spring, "Never Would Have Made It" by Marvin Sapp comes on. Now, I failed to mention that while all of this escorting stuff was going on, I was still running my growing brand management firm and faithfully attending church at First Rising Mt. Zion MBC on N Street NW. I was a certified heathen through and through.

Anyway, I take the exit and the song is blasting in the e-class Mercedes that I rented to run my escort errands. I'm legit singing at the top of my lungs as I pull up to the red stoplight. Then all of a sudden, I start feeling the sting of tears attack my eyes. Then, I heard God's voice so clearly:

"How dare you! How dare you do this to Me. After everything I brought you through? I've healed your body from cancer. I saved you from childhood rape and molestation. And this is how you repay Me?"

The tears fell and the light didn't change. I sat still for 7 minutes of God's wrath and rebuke with a repented heart and made up mind. It was time to leave this business alone. Following a series of events, God was very clear: I had to move to Sacramento, California in 4 days to start over. I didn't have much money; I left all of the escorting money with LaToya and I hadn't been collecting a check from my firm. I needed a sign. I told God that if these directions were from Him that my flight would be less than $300. I got on Expedia and found a flight from DC to Cali for $298 including tax. It was official - I was moving to the west coast.

A lot of things transpired after that move: I fell in love for the first time. It was clear that God had called me to be His prophet. I lost 96 pounds. I learned how to fast and pray. But overall, I got really close to God.

From 2014 to 2018 several events happened that push me further and further down the road to finding purpose. Throughout this book, I'll share a lot of personal stories that aided in this pursuit, but here are some milestone moments:

- 2014 - I lived in California and discovered that I was a prophet 🙀

- 2015 - I started producing Christian television and interim pastoring churches 🐺

- 2016 - Periscope got hot. I went viral for sharing my story about childhood trauma 😭

- 2017 - I found out the truth about my conception 💔

- 2018 - I was so lost, Google Maps couldn't find me 🗿

Although the season of running the escort service was a true catalyst for finding purpose (and my rock bottom), another moment was the straw that broke the camel's back. I've told this story dozens of times over the last couple of years, but it never gets old. Usually, I use it as a response when someone asks, "How did you become a millionaire?"

Around 2017, I started feeling so frustrated - borderline defeated - because I couldn't land on what my actual purpose was. I knew I was created to be more than a wife and mother. (Before you get spicy with me, I believe that being a wife and mom is an honorable profession. Yep. I even look at it as a profession. It takes a variety of skills to run a home and manage all of those tasks AND personalities. I just knew that it wasn't my sole purpose.) Anyway, I was irritated. I knew I had a great purpose of my own but I just couldn't pinpoint it.

My life started shifting around January 2019. Honestly, that may have been the best month of my life. My man and I had just gotten back together, I was living in Nashville and I was finally happy. Like REALLY happy. I had a real sense of peace and I was excited about what seemed like the natural next steps in my life. Let me tell you; 2019 was the year that God showed me that He was totally in control.

At this point, I'm living my best life but there's a constant nagging inside of me. I prayed and asked God to show me what I was supposed to be doing with my life. Almost immediately, (like literally the next morning) God started responding, but of course, it was in ways I didn't want to receive. He had my spiritual little sister call me and share that God had a plan for me beyond my marriage. That I was special. That I was called. Blah. Blah. Blah. In hindsight, it was what I needed at the time, but I was annoyed. That all was followed by a prophetic word via text from my man saying that God had a plan for me (again * insert eye roll here *) and that He was preparing me for the flood that was about to hit. Cool. Cool. I hated it.

Time was passing me by. I looked up and it was May 2019. I was praying fervently about my purpose and God was treating me like a redheaded stepchild in a reprobate family. Then one night in June, I heard it: EXILE. I just knew He wasn't talking to me. From my understanding, exile was for the disobedient and I wasn't that. In fact, I was doing all the things: fasting,

praying, tithing, sowing, studying - all the things. But exile kept showing up like dust bunnies in a well-kept home. You know how you clean your house every week, but somehow the dust just keeps showing up? Yep - that was exile.

In the middle of a 40-day no food fast, God told me I was moving to Mexico. Umm...no. There was no way I was moving to Mexico. First of all, I'm from San Antonio, but my Spanish was mad rusty. Second, is the water clean? Third, where Ima stay? Looking back now, God was setting me up for an Abram to Abraham experience. I was leaving the land of my kindred to go to a place God had already prepared for me.

I had a meeting with my prayer team and shared that God was sending me into exile. No one believed it. We spent hours tossing around the bible stories of people in exile. "Well, we all know Jonah was outta here," someone said. "Eh..he kinda just ran away," I replied. "Okay, well the children of Israel were exiled to the wilderness for 40 years. They were disobedient though," Enoch noted. Little did they know, I too was disobedient. God had been telling me to get back into business consulting for over a year, but I wanted to keep working as a stylist. Fashion was fun and being a consultant was stuffy.

Reluctantly, I followed God's instructions:

- Pack up everything you own and put it in storage.

- Travel to Atlanta and stay there for 7 days. You'll need to establish spiritual authority there.

- Book a one-way flight to Cancun.

- Stay in Mexico until I tell you otherwise.

It was a lot! By the second week of September, I was in Cancun. Let me be clear - this wasn't hotel zone Cancun where you go for Spring Break.

Nah. This wasn't palm trees, margaritas, and white sand. I lived in Cancun Cancun (Supermanzana or Region 239 to be exact). Within a week of me living there, the cartel had burned down my local nail shop in a turf war. I just couldn't understand why I had to be back in the hood that I had worked so hard to escape as a child in San Antonio. But time reveals all.

About a month into my exile, God allowed me to move into a nicer region and a gated condominium community. He gave me grace because I was finally starting to surrender. I had spent the greater part of 2019 arguing with everyone from my man to my Apostle and my friends about going back into business consulting. I finally told God that I would do it if he sent me a client who would change my mind.

In mid-October, I got an email from a headhunter on Facebook asking if I wanted to interview for a position as a project manager for a YouTuber with nearly one million subscribers. Reluctantly, I booked the interview. I had no desire to work on YouTube at all, but I needed to start making some money. After a series of interviews, I got hired for the job. The client was really sweet and ambitious which encouraged me to work harder for her. Four weeks later, she let me know that her channel views and Google AdSense revenue had doubled. "Who are you FOR REAL?" she asked. I laughed but I heard the Lord. "Tell her you're a business consultant." An hour or so later, we were laughing and talking about me coming to Toronto to help her prepare her mental health clinic to scale.

I walked away from that call both nervous and excited. Did I have the skills necessary to work with this client beyond a YouTube channel? What would it be like living in Toronto? As I walked to the market to get my groceries for the week, I felt a very gentle breeze tickle the nape of my neck and then it happened - I had an open vision. I saw the Lord as a pillar of fire in the middle of Quintana Roo Avenue (at first I thought y'all's cousins were burning some chicken or goat). I looked up in the sky and the clouds parted like the red sea, allowing the sun to pour through the heavens into the pillar of fire I saw on the ground. I heard the voice of God say, "Today, I'm renewing my covenant with you." Then like a flood, I watched the promises of God that had been spoken over my life flowing down the avenue. Tears fell from my eyes as I grabbed a cart and entered Soriana. I popped my AirPods in and silently worshipped while I gathered my produce. God had renewed His covenant with me and I was in good standing because I obeyed. My obedience allowed me to escape the 3-month exile.

On January 5, 2020, I started Kendra, Scale My Business in the Toronto Pearson International Airport and literally, the rest is history.

What became so clear was that God had called me to help motivate and inspire others to align themselves with God's plan for their lives. That call came with the requirement of aligning myself with His plan for Kendra's life first. Through this journey, I've learned that God-given purpose isn't linear. There isn't one straight and narrow path to uncovering God's perfect plan for your life. It's a journey.

Let's embark on your journey now.

01 It's the [Purpose] Principle, oh oh oh...

While your story may not be as dramatic as mine (did you read the Introduction?), I guarantee you that you'll have to walk through a specific process to fully find purpose. I don't know why you bought this book. Maybe you're really lost and desperate to find your way (good). Maybe you heard me speak somewhere and you just picked it up to support me (thank you). Maybe you think you know what your purpose is but you're open to see if it all adds up (equally good). Maybe you're just nosey (fine). Regardless, this process is going to cause you to unlearn what you think you know and surrender to some difficult memories as well as some new ideas.

This entire process came from those 7 years of being lost in the "wilderness." When I stepped back to process the journey, I noticed there were 5 major steps that I had to take to find my footing. We'll consistently revisit these steps throughout our work together:

THE PURPOSE PRINCIPLES

1. REFLECT ON **PASSION AND PAIN**

This is when we do the inner work and start understanding what we love, what brings us joy, peace, and fulfillment. These could be hobbies, passions, or even your favorite parts of your current job. A lot of people think that their passion is their purpose, but passion just becomes the gasoline for your purpose.

In addition to considering your passions, you also have to examine your pain. What are the difficult things that have happened to you? As hard as it can be to rehash those experiences, dealing with the hard things will be a major part of this work. During this phase, areas that you thought were healed will be exposed and difficult truths will be faced.

Look at all of it! Take the time to truly evaluate every part of yourself.

2. EXPLORE **PEOPLE, PLACES, AND PROFESSIONS**

Purpose isn't all inward - at some point, you have to turn your attention to the outside world.

The first part of this is understanding and accepting all of the things you DO NOT KNOW. You'll have to learn to be okay with not knowing things. There are so many different professions and industries out there, that you don't know about, or even understand. This is a great place to tap into mentorship both spiritually and professionally. Find a mentor or someone you can talk to who is already on the path, or in the place you want to be. Figure out if they align with you, and ask for guidance on your own path.

The second part of this is to try new things. You need to expose yourself to different people, places, and experiences. This will help you understand what you really resonate with in the world around you.

3. MAKE **IT PLAIN**

Writing down your purpose and all your discoveries around it is a really great way to help you walk in it. This practice will help you narrow down things that don't align with you and highlight the things that do. This is where purpose really starts to focus.

You'll find that as you begin to actually document your passions, your points of alignment, and your journey to purpose, God starts to provide clarity. We often think that we can manage all of the thoughts around purpose in our heads, but documenting it through journaling, vlogging, etc. will actually help you get down to your actual purpose statement.

4. DEVELOP **A PLAN**

So you've figured out what you like and don't like, you've started to meet new people, experience new things, and you may even have a mentor guiding you. What's next? Make a plan!

How are you going to fulfill your purpose? You don't have to know every single detail, but at this point, you are able to eliminate certain things, and probably have a pretty good idea of what you should be doing. How are you going to get there? Write it all down, and make it make sense. It's okay if things don't go exactly as planned - you will learn that your purpose will keep evolving. You'll want to have some sort of grasp on your purpose and the steps to arriving there.

5. WALK IN **PURPOSE**

You can go your entire life thinking about purpose, wondering when it's going to show up, and really just moving on without it. I cannot stress this part enough. If you have gotten to this stage, **don't let it go!** Once you've made your plan, MOVE! As you start taking the steps towards fulfillment, doors will open that you couldn't have even anticipated. So enjoy the journey!

Take this space to write about the factor in The Purpose Principles that you fear the most. Yep, let's tackle the fear. What are you afraid of? Why does this step scare you? What can you do right now to get ahead of the fear?

_____

_____

_____

_____

_____

_____

_____

_____

_____

_____

_____

_____

_____

_____

_____

_____

_____

_____

02 And Now You're Tryna Make Me Feel a Way... On Purpose

I've had a lot of jobs in my life. All jobs that could've been full careers, honestly. When I was 19 years old, I was the youngest full-time staffer on Capitol Hill. I was a freshman at Howard University (HU! You know!) majoring in political science. The reason I went to Howard was to be able to be in the mix of the politicos. I had known from a very young age that I wanted to be a politician and there was no better place to go to college than the seat of government. After working for two consecutive years on The Hill, I discovered that I actually wanted nothing to do with politics on the federal level. I spent my first 4 months interning for my hometown Congressman where I was solely responsible for answering the phones and opening mail. An opportunity opened up in a California Congressman's office as a Staff Assistant and I jumped on the chance to be a full-time staffer with a salary and 401K. It was one of the most challenging experiences of my life as I was juggling going to school full-time and working in one of the most competitive environments in the industry.

I left Capitol Hill to take a job with the UNCF as a legislative/legal assistant. I worked in two departments doing the job of two people: in the legal department, I assisted the general counsel with trusts and estates while helping with board governance. In the legislative office, I worked as an aid and lobbyist for minority education which put me back in the hallowed halls of Congress. Two more years elapsed and I was ready to leave. There were so many things I was battling working at UNCF from internal conflicts to my 4 hours each way commute. I interviewed for the "job of a lifetime" and moved to Texas.

Google left much to be desired overall. While I won't diverge the horrid details of my 6-month stint with the organization, I WILL say that being a minority at the company was very difficult. Not only was I a minority, but I was also a woman who was in charge of my own team. Between the good ole' boy games and the sabotage happening in my own pod, I knew that this was NOT it.

Off to the San Antonio Spurs organization where I came in to do ticket sales. I've never been into sports, so I knew this would have to be short-lived. Eight months later, I resigned from the Spurs and went full-time into my own business (I'll tell you about that in Chapter 12). FINALLY, I had landed on my purpose.

WRONG! The very hard lesson that I learned over the next 9 years is that purpose is not a profession or a job title. Your purpose is not to BE a thing. Your purpose is to DO a thing.

I hate to burst your bubble, but your purpose is not your job title. So it doesn't matter if you're a CEO, a teacher, a lawyer, or a salesperson - that's not your actual purpose. I don't care if you're the Director of HR or a custodian in a building, your purpose can't be boiled down to a single profession.

I want you to take a moment and think about what purpose means to you. Jot your thoughts below.

_____

_____

_____

_____

_____

_____

_____

_____

the reason for which something is done or created or for which something exists

So, why are we here? Why were we as individuals created? Why do we exist? Understand that tapping into the answer to these questions will reveal God's divine plan for your life.

Crazy enough, purpose isn't really about you. We often assume that we are here to fulfill something for ourselves, or that our purpose is specifically about us as individuals. What if I told you that purpose is actually about others? That what you do, and what you are meant to do here is for, and has a direct effect on the people around you? It's time to change your perception.

PERCEPTION: noun \ pər-ˈsep-shən \

the state of being or process of becoming aware of something through the senses

Most often, you're considering purpose as solely an internal destination. While purpose does initially begin as an introspective journey, it also includes an external discovery. We have to take the time to see what is happening inside of ourselves while also seeing the outside world through a different lens.

Your purpose is the answer to someone ELSE's problem. Don't believe me? If you peep the text in Genesis 2:18 KJV, this idea becomes clear. "And the Lord God said, It is not good that the man should be alone..." While we usually only attest this to the need for a spouse, God proves His point over and over throughout the bible that we are to serve each other in order to complete the work of the kingdom and glorify God.

- **We were liberated from sin to help others** - "For you have been called to live in freedom, my brothers and sisters. But don't use your freedom to satisfy your sinful nature. Instead, use your freedom to serve one another in love." Galatians 5:13 NLT

- **Nothing you do is supposed to be solely for you** - "Do nothing out of selfish ambition or vain conceit. Rather, in humility value others above yourselves, not looking to your own interests but each of you to the interests of the others." Philippians 2:3-4 NIV

- **Our service towards others has a reward** - "God is not unjust; he will not forget your work and the love you have shown him as you have helped his people and continue to help them." Hebrews 6:10 NIV

Let's take a moment to brainstorm. Consider the following questions:

What do people usually reach out to you for? What's a problem you seem to always solve?

_____

_____

_____

_____

_____

_____

What's a subject or topic people always approach you about?

_____

_____

_____

_____

_____

_____

03 Can We Talk for a Minute?

A big part of finding the answer to purpose is something I've talked about a lot recently, and that's "Consulting the Creator." If I want to know why something is made, I'll only know by asking the person who made it. Let's talk creators.

In 2021, I taught a class on money mindset to about 20 people. Somehow, trying to come out of a poverty mindset turned into a discussion around purpose so in the middle of that class, God gave me a revelation.

Meet my mentee, Cristina. Cristina makes bonnets. They're the best bonnets in the world (in my opinion); they're adjustable and satin on the inside and the outside. They're really the most amazing bonnets. Though we have a general idea, no one else can tell us exactly what the bonnets are made for. If you just saw it laying on a table, you might think it's just a piece of satin fabric or a beret. Now, Cristina communicates the purpose of her bonnets every single day on social media. How can we find our purpose if we aren't connected to the creator who created it on a regular basis? (SN: We get weird about communicating with God every day for various reasons. Sometimes it's because we're lazy, or we just don't get any results quick enough, so we quit. How can we understand what He wants from us if we don't communicate?).

Back to the bonnets; it takes regularly watching Cristina on social media to understand the full span of her bonnets. In addition, I've learned so much about natural haircare just from observing her daily, and with every post she makes, I better understand the purpose of the product I purchased even better. When I initially bought the product, I just wanted to support my mentee as a young, black college student. Then when I got it, I noticed how soft and luxurious it was. Then I wore it and it didn't come off of my head in my sleep (which is rare because every bonnet I've ever owned ends up in the abyss by the morning).

For months, I continued to watch Cristina every day. One day she said, "Did you know that your beauty supply store 'satin bonnet' isn't satin on the inside?" Wait a minute…WHAT? She follows that up with, "Yeah the outside of the 'satin bonnet' is satin, but the inside is polyester. So the part that is touching your hair is actually just ripping and rubbing your hair out. My bonnets are double satin-lined…" #MindBlown. I was shook because outside of being adjustable, I thought Cristina's bonnet was just like any other bonnet on the market.

Obviously, this isn't about bonnets. It's about how we get more intel from God about our own purpose. When it comes to Cristina, sometimes I'm talking to her about her bonnets, but most times she's talking to me (via her social posts). With all of the noise on social media, sometimes I even have to go seek her and look up her account to see what's new. God gives us all of these great gifts and great talents, but if we don't ask Him why we'll never fully understand the depth of His creation.

It's just not possible to know what you're supposed to be without consult- ing the Creator who made you and predestined your purpose. It's during time spent with God that we discover why we were placed on this earth. Much like the story about Cristina, we find out about all of our capabilities and "features" when we lean into God's divine knowledge. As you stay in constant communication with Him, He starts telling you that you're not like the other "bonnets." You learn over time that you're also double-sat- in lined, adjustable, and unmoveable. Plus, you're high quality because you're hand-crafted. Whew!

Now you might be saying, "Kendra! I've prayed. I've asked. I've con- sulted. And I've received nothing." I'm willing to bet all $6M+ I made in Kendra, Scale My Business that God HAS indeed spoken to you about your purpose. Personally, God gives me extreme clarity in my dreams. If I dream something, you can take it to the bank. If I see you getting married in a dream, buy your gown. If God shows me a tornado hitting a city, look for shelter. When it comes to my own business, I usually spend time in prayer, and then days, sometimes weeks later, the response shows up in my sleep.

Consulting God can look like various things. Honestly, it takes time to figure out what works best for you. I'm going to share the 7 ways that God shares revelation with us.

PRAYER

This may seem like a very obvious one, but one of the best ways to hear from God is through prayer. Prayer is just a way to communicate with God - it's like picking up the telephone. If you feel intimidated, just put on some worship music and sit still. Clear your mind of tedious thoughts and just let it flow. It may feel weird at first, but trust me, He will meet you where you are. Make sure you engage your active listening skills. The same way you pause and listen to a person when you're having a conversation, you'll need to do the same with Him. Allow yourself to lean into His presence and talk about everything. Here are some prayer points for you to use:

- Lord, I know that you made me in Your image and likeness. Can you reveal what you created me to do?

- I feel confused about what I was created for - I know that Your word says that You are not the author of confusion, but peace. Please let the peace that surpasses all understanding overtake me as I seek You for purpose.

- I know that You know the plans that You have for me. I trust You. Please reveal the part of the plan that I need to know right now so I can obey Your instructions.

- God, I need clarity around my purpose. Please speak to me in a way that I understand.

For some people, writing just comes naturally. If that's you, then start here with a fresh journal. Find some time to get still and jot down your prayers. Being able to get your thoughts and questions down on paper is a great way to engage with God. Not only does this provide you with a tangible space, but it also serves as a great reminder of answered prayers. As time goes by, you'll find that the things you write down begin to manifest in real life. Make sure that you take the time at the end of your journaling period to sit still and listen for the voice of God. Don't just slam your notebook closed and move on. Here are some prompts that can get you started:

- When I think about purpose, I feel _____.

- When I was a child, I loved to _____.

- The most important thing to me is _____.

- I feel most alive when I _____.

- I feel most connected to God when _____.

- I want my legacy to be _____.

WORSHIP

In all transparency, this is the toughest activity for me to complete. I struggle with being vulnerable with myself and with God, so He keeps pushing me into worship time in the mornings. Find yourself a good worship playlist (I have one that I created on Spotify, but sometimes I use prophetic worship instrumentals on YouTube), shut everything and everyone out, and just focus on God. As with every other point of revelation, make sure that you make time to just sit still and listen for God's voice. Here are some of my favorite worship songs for prayer:

- Yahweh x Matthew Stevenson

- You Always Hear Me x Valencia Lacy

- I Surrender x Psalmist Raine

- Glory to the Lamb x Geoffrey Golden

- Just Want You x Travis Greene

STUDYING

In contrast, studying is my FAVORITE way to get revelation. I can literally get lost in the bible for hours and hours *cue Muni Long's track*. If you don't know where to start, I recommend beginning with the first chapter of the book of Jeremiah; it's about God calling young Jeremiah to be a prophet. While you may not be a prophet, the mental and emotional anguish Jeremiah faces is very similar to the way we feel when we don't know our own purpose.

When it comes to studying, I have a very specific method that has helped me gain the most revelation. Trust me, studying like this is a game-changer!

- Read the chosen verse in your favorite version of the bible (I usually use the King James Version or the New International Version).

- Read that same verse in another version (I like the Amplified Version, New Living Translations, and English Standard Version).

- Now, use the Merriam-Webster dictionary to look up the keywords. ESPECIALLY words that you think you know the meaning of.

- Combine all of those things and go back to the original version - what is the new information or revelation that you have now?

I'll do one verse as an example. Let's take a look at Jeremiah 1:5 KJV:

> "**Before** I formed thee in the belly I knew thee, and before thou camest forth out of the womb I sanctified thee, and I ordained thee a prophet unto the nations."

Now let's look at the same verse in the NLT:

> "I knew you **before** I formed you in your mother's womb. Before you were born I set you apart and appointed you as my prophet to the nations."

Let's also use the AMP:

> "**Before** I formed you in the womb I knew you [and approved of you as My chosen instrument], And before you were born I consecrated you [to Myself as My own]; I have appointed you as a prophet to the nations."

We've already received a lot more understanding, but let's get into a couple of definitions (in my own time, I would definitely be looking up a LOT more words than these, but I want to be concise):

BEFORE: adverb or adjective \ bi-ˈför , bē- \

in advance; ahead

AHEAD: adverb or adjective \ ə-ˈhed \

in, into or for the future

FUTURE: adjective \ ˈfyü-chər \

of, relating to, or constituting a verb tense expressive of time yet to come

YET: adverb \ ˈyet \

at a future time: EVENTUALLY

EVENTUALLY: adverb \ i-ˈven(t)-sh(ə-)wə-lē \

at an unspecified later time: in the end

Multiple things that we learned here just from looking up ONE word (this is a revelation):

- He had a plan for you from the very beginning. He prepared for you.

- You shouldn't be discouraged if your purpose hasn't become clear YET. In the end, it will be revealed and you will walk in it. When you do eventually walk in your purpose, know that He already made every provision your needed.

I'll spare you the full study, but from this verse alone, I gleaned that God made Himself acquainted with you in advance of you even being born. He has a specified time, place, people, and purpose for you - there are people who are called to you! And you are preferred by Him to be used as His tool. With that, you have benefits AND help. Whew! If this didn't inspire you to get in that bible, then IDK what will.

DREAMS + VISIONS

As I mentioned before, this is currently the most accurate way that I understand God's plan for my life. Believe it or not, I actually dreamed of the cover for this book. I took a midday nap one day and saw myself signing books with this very cover! So, yes! God does speak to us in our dreams. Now, don't get it twisted - there are dreams that you have because you ate some bacon before you fell asleep or you watched a horror movie and now you're tripping in a forest. Over time, it will become clear what dreams are just your own vain imaginations versus things that God wants you to see. Just keep dreaming! Here are a few tips about getting to the bottom of your dreams:

- Name, date, and title your dream, record your waking time. Daniel 7:1 NKJV says,"...Daniel had a dream and visions of his head while on his bed. Then he wrote down the dream, telling the main facts." (Sidenote: PLEASE sleep in your bed. If you're a couch sleeper, you need to break that habit).

- Write or draw your dream out in bullet points, diagrams, outlines, or paragraph form. I usually just voice-record the dream so I can revisit it when I'm fully awake.

- Record the main facts and eliminate the unnecessary details

- Ask the Holy Spirit for insight and understanding of the dream in prayer.

- Does the dream symbol appear in the Bible? Search it out in the Word. Dreams from the Lord will never go against His word. (Proverbs 25:2)

- Look for the theme or essence the dream is communicating to you. Relate the dreams to your circumstances. Consecutive dreams often have the same or similar meaning (Genesis.41:1-7, 25-31). God will often speak the same message more than once.

- Visualize the dream as you recall or rehearse the main symbols in the scenes of the dream. I usually pay attention to the colors, numbers, main symbols, and emotions. Were you scared in the dream? Did you wake up anxious?

When understanding and interpreting dreams, remember that God sent the Holy Spirit for moments like this. John 14:26 ESV says, "But the Helper, the Holy Spirit, whom the Father will send in My name, He will teach you all things, and bring to your remembrance all that I, said to you."

AUDIBLE SPEECH

Yes, God speaks with a voice. Now, it may not happen for you immediately, but as you continue to inquire about your purpose, God's voice becomes clearer. A lot of people become frustrated when they're listening for His voice, but God chin-checked me like Mike Tyson vs. Evander Holyfield a long time ago. I was on the phone with a friend one night and she was venting about not being able to hear God's voice. As she was going on and on, the Lord gave me a word for her. "God said that He comes in a small, still voice because He won't compete with the noise of your life." The word hit so hard, that it took MY breath away.

God is always trying to communicate with us: He's in the wind, the music, the stars - everything. But He's never going to fight for your attention. When you allow yourself to get still, He'll show up. The more you commune with Him, the easier it is to hear His voice.

UNCTIONS

This may be one of the more cryptic forms of revelation-getting, but some people have veryyyyyy strong feelings that are God-led. Some people call it intuition, but it's God-tuition. When someone receives an unction, what's actually happening is that the Holy Spirit is engaging in an exchange. They are sporadic, unplanned, and unexpected, but when you receive them, an unction is an irrevocable truth.

1 John 2:20 DARBY sheds some biblical light on this: "And *ye* have [the] unction from the holy [one], and ye know all things."

It's also important to note that God speaks to us differently in different seasons of our lives. Right now, God may easily respond to your petitions and inquiries when you're in worship because it's your comfort zone (usually very emotional people find worship easy). In the next season, God may choose to show you things when you're studying the word. On the flip side, if you find yourself receiving revelation from studying your bible (usually analytical people lean into studying), God may lead you to journal for answers.

Time for your exercise. I want you to think back to the last 4-6 months of your life. How have you felt God communicating with you? Are there any notable things He's shared with you about your purpose?

_____

_____

_____

_____

_____

_____

_____

_____

_____

_____

_____

_____

_____

_____

_____

_____

_____

_____

_____

Now, take a moment and pray RIGHT NOW. While the teaching on revelation is fresh in your mind, take advantage of your opportunity to ask Him for details about your unique characteristics, skills, and gifts. Ask Him to show you more concerning your purpose and jot your notes down here.

_____

_____

_____

_____

_____

_____

_____

_____

_____

_____

_____

_____

_____

_____

_____

_____

_____

_____

_____

_____

04 Passionate From Miles Away

Now that I'm out of my Wayland Baptist Theological Seminary bag, let's talk about some practical things we can do to keep moving closer and closer to the discovery of purpose.

I knew I wanted to work in the fashion industry when I was about 10 years old. I had moved into a house in the hood (more on that later) with my stepgrandmother, Lillie Mae. Sis. Lillie, as she was affectionately called, was the church's treasurer and Sunday School superintendent - plus, she was the choir's lead tenor. Every Saturday night, Lillie would plan out her look for church on Sunday morning. Mostly because we had to be out the door at 8:30 am, but also because she was a fashionista in her own right. Lillie was the first woman I ever saw who did ALL the things when she got dressed - pantyhose, girdle, bra, camisole, suit, jewelry, AND perfume. Prior to living with her, I only saw my mom get dressed up on super special occasions and she NEVER wore a girdle.

Lillie taught me how to pick a color out of a printed garment in order to find the right accessories. I have so many memories of Saturdays spent walking McCreless or Windsor Park Mall looking for the perfect outfit for Sundays at Holy Nation Baptist Church. On rare occasions, usually Easter or Christmas, we would make the 30-minute drive north to Rolling Oaks Mall to find the perfect pastel dresses or green suits for our big day. Lillie made me feel like the most beautiful girl in the church just because of how she dressed me. As I got older, I got to pick out my own clothes and she would critique my look with a smug, "That looks okay," or a direct, "Girl! You ain't going out the house looking like that!" She truly shaped the way I felt about fashion and I quickly learned that clothes could shift the way others judged you, but more importantly, how you judged yourself.

By the time I was 16, Lillie Mae was asking me for fashion advice. "No, Nana. That necklace doesn't go with that jacket," I'd remark while laying across her bed eating a bowl seedless of grapes. Reluctantly, she'd go back to her armoire and swap the short gold chain necklace for a beaded strand. It never failed; whatever I had her change was the thing that she got the most compliments on after service. I really just wanted my Nana to feel the same way that she made me feel - beautiful.

That's how I landed in the fashion industry nearly 15 years later. I was about to turn 30 and I had grown bored with my own consulting business. I ended up selling that business to my then COO and starting The Modern Disciple - a styling and creative direction business that was geared towards helping women feel their very best every day. Although this career was fulfilling my childhood dream of working in fashion, I had to step back and examine my work: was making women feel beautiful through clothes something God wanted me to fully pursue as purpose or was it just one of my own passions?

Purpose is often confused with passion and although you might fulfill your ultimate purpose through your passion, there is a distinct difference between the two.

How would you describe passion?

_____

_____

_____

_____

_____

_____

_____

a strong liking or desire for or devotion to some activity, object, or concept

Passion is really all about emotions. We're usually motivated to pursue something that we're passionate about because it feels good. Passions (much like emotions), come and go because they're kind of all over the place. Today you could be passionate about making espresso and tomorrow you could detest anything with caffeine. You could be super passionate about preserving the environment today and then buying fast fashion tonight. Passions are mainly things we internally feel good about and they usually have more of a focus on us. For example, you could be passionate about listening to music, making art, playing sports, reading books, writing blog posts - the list goes on and on.

Purpose has more of a clear and well-defined focus. Purpose could be categorized as the "why" or the reason that we do what we do. Remember, your purpose is not for you. It's really about the impact that you have on others and the world around you. While passions can be fleeting, your purpose is a long-term, constant thing.

For example, your purpose could be to empower, heal and lead a generation. You could use your passion for music to do all of those things. You could use your passion for writing to create awareness or make certain connections that will aid in the empowerment of others. Your passion for reading could help you learn more about healing the people you're called to. What you'll find on your journey is that you will need to use your passions to fuel your purpose.

We often have the biggest impact when we are able to align our passions with our purpose versus making them compete or choosing passion over purpose. In that sense, our purpose becomes a lot more emotionally fueled, allowing us to keep filling our tank with what we need to be productive and successful. We expand our reach, increase our speed, and achieve our accomplishments when we combine our passions with our purpose.

Let's dig a little deeper into passions. Remember that passions are about you! What makes you feel good? What fulfills you? Think about that as you respond to each question.

Write down all of the things you LOVE doing. What makes you happy? What motivates you?

What feels good? Put one thing on each line and don't stop until you fill them all in.

_____   _____

_____   _____

_____   _____

_____   _____

_____   _____

_____   _____

List things that come EASY to you. Consider things you don't even have to really think about.

_____   _____

_____   _____

_____   _____

_____   _____

_____   _____

_____   _____

_____   _____

If you could only do one of those activities for the rest of your life, which one would you choose?

Your ONE thing (we'll call this your Golden Spoon):

_____

How would that make you feel?

_____

_____

_____

_____

_____

_____

_____

_____

05

Joy and PAIN.
Like Sunshine and RAIN.

You probably just cringed at the thought of talking about your pain. I get it. I used to hate talking about (pssh, THINKING about) the painful experiences I've had in my life. Unfortunately, part of that internal discovery process is not just talking about your passions, but also tackling your pain. (trigger warning: death and sexual assault).

I was 8 years old when my best friend died. It was November 27, 1995. I woke up crying in a cold sweat. This wasn't uncommon. At that young age, I didn't know it, but I was a prophet. I had experienced a lot of supernatural things as a child from seeing spirits in our home to sharing things that were futuristic that ultimately came to pass. In 1996, I even dreamt about the TWA Flight 800 plane crash the night before it happened.

My mom came into my room to wake me up for school. I was lying flat on my back when the tears started to fall onto my Little Mermaid sheets. "I don't feel good, Mommy." The lie made its way out of my mouth before I could think twice. I knew that my mom had a soft spot for me, especially when I was sick. "What's the matter, baby? Is it your head? Your stomach? Your chest?" my mom asked as she felt my face with the back of her hand. Though I had lied just a moment before, I couldn't keep the lie going and my mom saw right through it. "Kendra. Tell me what's wrong." I sat in silence. "Baby, please tell me what's wrong. Did you have a bad dream?" I slowly nodded my head as I sat up and pulled my knees to my chest. I needed all of the comfort I could get. After a few more quiet moments, I finally caught my breath and blurted out, "Gammy's gonna die!"

Although my Gammy was going to have a small outpatient procedure that day, there was nothing wrong with her - or so we thought. My mom replied, "No she's not, baby. She'll be fine." I kept shaking my head because I knew what I saw in my dreams. Even at that age, I was having 6-8 dreams per night. Somewhere between playing Donkey Kong on Nintendo and eating Skittles, my dreams shifted to me holding a funeral program that read, "Jeraldine Leeper Hill" with a beautiful black and white photo of my Gammy. I snapped out of the vision that was replaying in my mind when my mom said that I could stay home from school and go with her to Beach Pavillion at Ft. Sam Houston to accompany Gammy.

The events that occurred between that moment and Gammy's death are a blur. Even now as I sit with my thoughts, I can't remember what happened. All I know is that we were sitting in the waiting room when the doctor and the chaplain came in. I knew it was over and I started crying as my mom and I walked to the chaplain's tiny office. Sitting at a desk across from my mom, the chaplain told us the news. Gammy died. Her procedure went well but when they put her in the elevator, she went from laughing and joking to suffering a heart attack.

Charles, my grandfather, came up to Beach Pavillion to meet us after Gammy's surgery. He was the life of the party in our family. Everybody loved him. He was the uncle who gave every kid money at family functions, the cousin who would play the dozens with ANYONE (and win), and the brother everyone could depend on. He was handsome, funny, and super charismatic. In his typical fashion, he entered the waiting room laughing and clowning around with everyone who was there. His jovial smile turned sour the moment a stranger extended their condolences to him. He stormed out to find my mom and inquire about what had happened. My mom was at the nurse's station when Charles walked up to her with a confused look on his face. "Marina, what's going on?" My mom froze. The moment was challenging for her. It was literally the hardest thing she would ever have to say to him. "I don't even know how to tell you this." He replied, "What?" My mom said, "Mama died today." He began to shake his head while saying, "No. No no no no. NO! No." He turned slowly and walked out of the building. Charles was destroyed.

Back at home, everything was dark. Gammy had a green thumb and she spent most of her day watching soap operas and tending to her plants. I actually can't recall a single morning where I got up and the house wasn't clean with the plants being watered and the blinds open to "let the Lord in." Everything after her death was the polar opposite and the house got darker and darker with each passing day. The crazy thing is that it wasn't just visually dark; it was spiritually dark too.

I don't even think 3 days had passed before Charles started molesting me. The first time it happened, my mom, Charles, and I were all sleeping in the master bedroom. Everyone had taken Gammy's death so hard so we tried to stay together as much as possible. I woke up one morning with Charles' fingers in my underwear. When I fully opened my eyes and looked at him, he used his other hand to silence me. It was understood that I wasn't allowed to speak on it.

Shortly after Gammy's funeral, I was taking a nap in my Little Mermaid ladened room when Charles came through my door. My mom had gone to spend some alone time with her then-boyfriend. I'll spare you the details, but the memory of Ariel swimming on the curtains, while Charles raped me, played over and over in my mind for years. Maybe that's because he continued to violate me for years. He made it clear that I wasn't ever supposed to tell my mom. "She won't believe you anyway," he would add to his remarks as he adjusted his pants.

#Pause. I know this is a lot to share, but I want you to know that if you have ever been a victim of sexual assault, it's not your fault. It's time to be free from the guilt and shame that comes with being a victim of rape and molestation. I know that you have probably thought a million things:

- What's wrong with me that someone would do that to me?

- What did I do to make them do this?

- What did I do to deserve being treated like this?

- I must have led them on.

- I probably said something that made them think it was okay.

- I deserved this.

- No one protected me. I must not be worthy of love and protection.

- I'll forever be damaged goods. No one will ever love me for real.

- I'm disgusting.

- I was being a slut.

- I guess it wasn't THAT bad.

There's a full range of emotions that passes through the mind of someone who bears the cross of sexual abuse. Again, YOU ARE WORTHY. YOU ARE LOVED. It was NOT YOUR FAULT.

I spent years in therapy as an adult to work through the residue of being raped by Charles. I also had to work through the way I felt about my mother. Even though I hadn't told her, I felt like she knew and just allowed me to be abused. She ended up getting married and seemingly moving on with her life while I was still suffering internally every single day. Little did I know, she too had been abused at the hands of Charles - her own dad. There are a lot of mental struggles and challenges that come with sexual abuse and honestly, I think my mom was just trying to escape the harsh reality that she had been taken advantage of by her biological father. My mom recently told me that she threatened Charles and told him that she would kill him if he ever touched me. I'm laughing now because back then I couldn't imagine my mom loving me so much - we were pretty distanced after she got married - but knowing what I know now, I understand that she really did love me very deeply and would've given her own life for me (thanks, Mommy!). Our lives were just very complicated.

Charles died 9 years after Gammy died - literally November 20, 2004. He had been sick for some time and was suffering a very slow and painful death. We're talking about a man who had worked as a U.S. Airforce mechanic for McDonnell Douglas to a shell of a man who had to wear diapers because his organs were shutting down one by one.

I was at University Interscholastic League (UIL) All-Region Choir practice at my high school. I think I placed like 5th chair as an Alto II that year. I had to read the introduction at our concert for a piece called "Sleep" by Eric Whitacre. Eerily enough, the song was written by Whitacre for a mezzo-soprano who commissioned the piece in memory of her parent who had died within weeks of each other after more than fifty years of marriage. As soon as we finished rehearsing the moody a cappella piece, a choir director took a microphone and said, "Kendra Hill. Kendra Hill, please report to the stage door." A bit confused, I reluctantly parted the sea of singers on the risers as I descended from the top row to head to the side of the stage. When I opened the door, my mom was standing outside, tears streaming down her face. Before I could ask what was wrong, she said, "Your Papa died." The scream that left my body didn't just curdle blood; it ricocheted through the outdoor breezeway, across the campus, and back into the auditorium where the choir was practicing. She continued, "He died, but they brought him back and the first thing he asked was 'where's Kendra?'" I was shook. This man had a do not resuscitate order, yet the doctors revived him. I knew that I had to go see him.

After I gathered myself and grabbed my belongings, we headed to the new Brook Army Medical Center (BAMC) at Ft. Sam. This military base didn't only house the place where my Gammy died (and Charles was about to die), but I was also born at the Old BAMC back in 1987. The ironic homecoming was sobering. I cried from my high school to the hospital room door. When I walked into Charles' room, all of my aunts, uncles, and cousins were assembled, laughing and crying at whatever joke he was telling. I remember him making some joke about my face being all torn up from crying before he made everyone leave.

Standing beside the bed of a dying rapist who I still had so much love and admiration for was a challenge. I couldn't rationalize my feelings. I was sad. Angry. Frustrated. Disappointed. Depressed. Excited. Yep - excited.

I couldn't stop the tears from falling all over his bed. I crawled into the tiny hospital bed with him to hear his heartbeat for what I knew would be the last time. Even though he had done so much to hurt me, he was still my Papa and his death was hurting more than I ever thought it would. He grabbed my hand and said, "Kendra, if I ever did anything to hurt you, I'm sorry." I was miffed at his half-hearted apology. "IF? IF??!" Before I knew it, the words were leaving my throat. He started to cry too. "I know I did things that hurt you. If you can forgive me…" his voice trailed off. He looked over at me with pleading eyes. A long moment passed before I spoke again. Internally, I was trying to wrap my mind around the revelation that was unfolding before my eyes.

Weeks prior, God had started speaking to me about forgiving Charles. I had recently accepted my call and been licensed in ministry so God was really on my case. He showed me how I had been harboring unforgiveness like the core of a rotting apple in an old lunchbox. I turned to Charles with a large volume of tears falling down my face. "I already did." He let out a loud sigh of relief and replied, "Good. God said He wouldn't receive me unless you did." As I was grappling with the absolute sovereignty of God, the sound of the door opening interrupted my thoughts. My family returned to also say their final goodbyes.

I kissed my Papa's bald head, then his cheek while squeezing his hand. "I love you, Papa," I whispered. "I love you too, Squirrel," he replied. I walked out of the room and straight to the elevator. I just needed some air. As I pressed the button and waited to be taken away by the lift, I heard the heart monitor flatline. My predator was dead.

While you're clutching your proverbial pearls, I want to explain why I shared all of this in such detail. The death of my Gammy and the subsequent abuse that followed are the first memories I have of true pain. Sure, I had scraped my knees on the playground (I feel like everybody who played outside has those Simba scars on their knees). I had gotten in trouble and been spanked by my mom. I had even suffered an anaphylactic shock from being stung by a bee. But nothing was as painful as that time period of my life. What I didn't understand then, but truly appreciate now, is that my pain produced power.

When I get up in front of a group of people and share my testimony about surviving rape as a child, women get set free. They find comfort in knowing that not only has someone else experienced the pain, shame, guilt, and embarrassment that they have, but they also have an example of life after rape. Back in 2016-2018 when I was traveling to preach and interim pastor churches, this one difficult part of my life that I endured was the service headliner. It didn't matter how well I preached the word, sang a hymn (did you know I can sang? lol), or carried on, the altar calls for men and women who had been sexually violated were the most powerful part of the service.

All of these experiences are a part of my purpose. It has been a challenging road, but it's necessary for what I have been called to do. Once you heal from something, it's time to take that pain and produce power that ultimately helps to drive purpose. If you haven't healed, it's difficult to speak from a place of power that shifts things in other people. Your spoken words can help move someone from a place of despair to a place of victory. Avoidance usually creeps up when having to address difficult situations in our lives, but no one benefits from evading your healing. You don't benefit long term because you're still carrying the weight and others don't get to hear your story and be inspired. Revelation 12:11 KJV is true: "And they overcame him by the blood of the Lamb, and by the word of their testimony…"

I want you to think back to some of your painful moments in life. I know that this can be challenging as we typically strive to archive the negative experiences of our past; however, painful experiences are necessary for your making. They help to shape and mold you into the person you need to be in order to fulfill your purpose and execute God's plan for your life. In the space below, I want you to jot down some painful experiences of your past that you have already worked through. Write down whatever comes to mind.

_____

_____

_____

_____

_____

_____

_____

Now - I want you to think about some of the painful memories that you haven't fully unpacked. While I know that this small workspace is not enough room to unleash all of the pain, it's at least a start. Feel free to tap into your journal if you need more space. What happened? How did it make you feel? What are some of the ways you have seen the impact of these experiences show up in your life now?

_____

_____

_____

_____

_____

_____

_____

It's This One Thing

We've covered (and uncovered) a lot over the last few chapters, so I just want to remind you to trust the process. I know that you may have had to face some challenging things from mindset shifts and transformations to unearthing some raw emotions, but know that this is going to help you gain real clarity on your purpose. Sometimes it has to get a little messy before we can get to a masterpiece.

Here's a messy story for you: it was March 2020 and I was living in Toronto Canada. I have been working with the client from my time in Cancun that change my mind about being a consultant. A couple of weeks before everybody and everything in the world shut down, she and I went to an event for L'Oreal. As we were in the Uber leaving the event, I told her that I wanted to cut my hair. Of course, she didn't think anything of it because who would? But cutting my hair is something that I go through whenever there's a major change happening in my life. I remember telling her that I wasn't sure if it was a change for me or a change for other people, but I felt something really bad getting ready to happen.

Needless to say, the day that we shut down in Toronto, the client called me shook. She couldn't believe that my spidey senses picked up that something was coming that would have a negative impact on our lives. I spent the next few months in total isolation in my 500 square-foot condo that I rented through Airbnb. To say that it was lonely is an understatement. Because I had bronchitis as a condition, it was impossible for me to go out and even get fresh air or grab my groceries. I ended up having to hire an assistant (hey, Tre!) to do my grocery shopping and run my minimal errands. Of course, I wanted to come back home to the States, but the thought of getting on a flight was paralyzing. I couldn't imagine being on a crowded plane with hundreds of people while coronavirus was running rampant.

I don't need to belabor the point about the impact that the pandemic had on us in that first year, but I do need to emphasize what happened to me. The moment the quarantine started, I knew that God was going to do something that would blow my mind. At the end of 2019 while I was preparing to move to Toronto, one of my mentees texted me with a prophetic word:

DEC 08, 2019, 9:47 AM

Good morning. I had a dream about you. In the dream we met up and God was speaking to me about u. He said,"this is her year" and "she will be a millionaire ". Also His presence is with you. I saw you had a

Now how was God going to make me a millionaire when the whole world has shut down? I wasn't sure but for some reason, my faith pushed me into the next season of my life. While most business owners were panicking and trying to figure out how to Pivot, my business was flourishing. In the first week of the pandemic, my business made over $75,000 by helping other businesses develop contingency plans and handbooks for remote work. On top of that, God was speaking to me like crazy. I definitely accredit this to the fact that I was spending so much time with him, but for some reason, His voice was so clear during this season. I felt led to start a new division in my business for YouTubers. This space allowed me to develop and manage the business side of creators' careers. Though I wasn't completely sure how it would work, I move that God was leading me in that direction.

We took on a few YouTube clients between April and June, but in July 2020, we officially launched the division for YouTubers. On July 24th, we hit 1 million dollars in revenue. What started off as a very messy season turned into one of the greatest times of my life. I discovered very quickly that my Golden Spoon was helping people solve problems. and even though I wasn't clear on my full purpose statement, that discovery was just around the corner.

People think of purpose as something you have to search for, when in fact, your purpose is already within you. I've legit been solving people's problems my whole life. It's really just a process of uncovering purpose and then aligning yourself with God's plan and timing to find success. We just have to figure out what He wants us to do.

What was your Golden Spoon from Chapter 4?

Your Golden Spoon:

Now that you know your Golden Spoon, we can go a little deeper and get closer to our purpose statement. Your Golden Spoon and your purpose may not be the same thing, but if you're able to focus on one thing that you're passionate about and needed for, it makes the process a lot easier. Here are 7 proven steps you can use to get closer to your purpose:

BE STILL, MY SOUL

Repeat after me: Stillness is a gift.

You have to learn how to get still. We have so many things happening around us every single day, but if the pandemic hasn't taught us anything, it's shown us what stillness looks like. Though things have picked back up and we're in our new normal, we have to remember what it was to sit down and be settled.

Psalm 46:10 AMP says, "Be still and know (recognize, understand) that I am God..." You have to actively work at stillness. Don't believe me? Let's look at this:

BE: verb \ ˈbē \

to equal in meaning: have the same connotation as: SYMBOLIZE

Synonyms: abide, continue, endure, hold on, hold up, keep (on), last, lead, persist, flourish, prosper, thrive

So the idea of "be" in this context literally means to have the same meaning as something. So you should *be* so still that you literally *symbolize* stillness. #Shook. Your stillness should be so that you actually embody and become stillness before God. This stillness not only honors the majesty of God but also allows you to recognize Him as the source of all actions.

STILL: adjective \ ˈstil \

devoid of or abstaining from motion

Antonyms: moving, active, stir up

Don't miss this: if we're still, then God has permission to move! And if He's moving, then He's also stirring up things within us (our gifts, passions, and talents) and outside of us (our doors, opportunities, and assignments). God's actions cause a reaction from us. So if He's moving and opening a door for you, then it would cause you to walk through that door. Stillness is just as much about honoring God as it is allowing Him to prepare the next space for you.

Stillness could look different in different times of our lives. I literally spent about 6 or 7 years avoiding television, so much so that I don't own a single TV! I literally just started watching Netflix and Hulu this year! Turn off your devices, music, and anything else that might distract you. If you live with others or have household responsibilities, create the routine of stillness and notify your people. Maybe you find an hour on Sundays to be still or maybe you have the privilege of seeking God through stillness every morning. Regardless of the frequency, the goal is to get quiet and just exist.

If you need to tap into hearing him right now, go back to Chapter 3 and review the section on audible speech. God is often talking to us but we need to practice listening. Our struggles with stillness (and silence) are a major part of the reason why God speaks to so many of us through our dreams - it's the only time a lot of us are still and quiet!

What can stillness look like for you right now? Map out your plan to be still and quiet this week.

_____

_____

_____

_____

_____

_____

_____

_____

TAP TAP TAP INTO THE WORD, SAWEETIE!

The best way to learn what God's voice sounds like is to read His word. We don't mind putting aside an hour to talk to our friends or scroll through Instagram (*cough* or spend hours scrolling TikTok *cough*). But how much further along would you be in your relationship with God and pursuit of purpose if you put that same time into communing with the Lord?

Multiple things happen when you actually get in your bible. Not only do you become more familiar with His voice, but you also gain clarity concerning His intentions for your life. Jeremiah 29:11 AMP is clear, "For I know the plans and thoughts that I have for you,' says the Lord, 'plans for peace and well-being and not for disaster, to give you a future and a hope." There's already a pre-determined plan in store for you. It's up to you to get in your bible, become familiar with His voice, and do what He's telling you to do.

What has God been saying to you lately? How does your Golden Spoon fit into His plan?

_____

_____

_____

_____

_____

_____

_____

_____

_____

IT'S GRATEFULNESS

This is a big component when it comes to purpose. Gratitude unlocks the doors to abundance. When you're able to express gratitude to God, it activates your "Christian benefits package."

Let's look at Psalm 103:2-5 AMP: "Bless and affectionately praise the Lord, O my soul, and do not forget any of His benefits; Who forgives all your sins, Who heals all your diseases; Who redeems your life from the pit, Who crowns you [lavishly] with lovingkindness and tender mercy; Who satisfies your years with good things, So that your youth is renewed like the [soaring] eagle."

Our expression of gratitude towards God allows us to tap into a tonnnnn of advantages. That one scripture alone mentioned liberation from sin, healing of sickness, saving us from despair, extending love and empathy, and rejuvenation! And to think, that's just blessing God for being God. Imagine the extended package you could unlock by thanking Him for what you already have in and around you!

This concentrated journey for purpose has us evaluating our lives in ways we don't on a daily basis. It's easy to get caught up in what we don't have when we're being so future-focused. Take a moment to reflect. What are some things you have (internally and externally) that you're grateful for?

I keep saying it, and I'm gonna say it again: your purpose is not for you.

<u>IMPACT: noun \ 'im-ˌpakt \</u>

the force of impression of one thing on another: a significant or major effect

If your purpose is your impact then you have to consider how your purpose is used for other people. Nothing about who you were called to be or what you were created to do is about you – EVER!

It's my belief that relationship is the currency of Heaven. You're here for other people. You're not here for yourself and nothing that you experience or that you learn is solely for your own benefit. In other words, our relationships with others allow us to give and receive on a deeply spiritual level. What would be the point of life if we were only made to serve ourselves?

Consider this: List the last three experiences you've had using your Golden Spoon for others. When did these experiences occur and what was the result?

Experience 1

_____

_____

_____

_____

_____

_____

_____

Approximate Date

_____

_____

What was the result?

_____

_____

_____

_____

_____

_____

Experience 2

_____

_____

_____

_____

_____

_____

Approximate Date

_____

_____

What was the result?

_____

_____

_____

_____

_____

_____

_____

Experience 3

_____

_____

_____

_____

_____

_____

Approximate Date

_____

_____

What was the result?

_____

_____

_____

_____

_____

_____

_____

SPEND SOME TIME WITH ME

Now that you know the thing you are really most passionate about, it's time to commit to making some time doing what you love. This is a great way to further uncover your purpose. Often times our passions are what bring us joy. They fulfill us in a way that ultimately makes us better people.

Colossians 3:23-24 ESV says, "Whatever you do, work heartily, as for the Lord and not for men, knowing that from the Lord you will receive the inheritance as your reward. You are serving the Lord Christ." This is key when pursuing your passions or your Golden Spoon. Make sure that you keep God as the driving factor. If you chase your Golden Spoon for selfish ambition or self-gratification, you'll fail. Your Golden Spoon is about service to others and if you keep God as the foundation, you can't go wrong.

If we commit time to our passions, it becomes easier to find ways to align our passions with our purpose and have that much bigger of an impact.

What's one way you can integrate a commitment to your passions into your life?

_____

_____

_____

_____

_____

_____

Do you ever get feelings about things you can't explain? We have our instincts, but there are so many times we receive messages that come from outside of ourselves. Listen closely to your gut. Again, God is speaking to us in more ways than we recognize.

Oftentimes, we use our gut instinct, intuition, and discernment only in negative situations. It's like we only use our intuition to be negative. "Ooh, I can't trust this person." Or when you're walking down a dark alley and you're like, "Ooh, someone might jump out and get me!" It's a mindset shift to go into a place where you start tapping into that gift of intuition or discernment and attribute it to positive experiences.

We're all born with instincts. Everybody has those feelings that they can't shake. One thing I've learned is that I have to be open to whatever the Spirit of God is trying to reveal to me. Sometimes God is trying to get you to tap into your gut instinct to discern new ideas and opportunities that will have a positive impact on your life. Shift your mindset and start tapping into that gift for positive experiences and supernatural knowledge.

Reflect on a time when you know God gave you a divine message about something positive that was coming. It may take a second to come up with the scenario, but God is always giving us nudges for our good.

_____

_____

_____

_____

_____

_____

WE'RE ALL IN THIS TOGETHER *cue High School Musical*

Sometimes it takes other people to help direct us to our purpose. Find a group of like-minded people who can help get you where you are trying to go. Building connections help us learn things we didn't even think we needed to know. Again, relationship is the currency of Heaven.

This is literally the reason I created The Milli Club (my membership community). I was struggling to find faith-based entrepreneurs who were just as serious about their spiritual wealth as they were about their bank accounts. As I dug deeper into the internet, I realized that this space didn't exist and there were so many of my own followers looking for the exact same thing. What came out of that season is a group of people that study the bible together, work together, get money together, and more.

God cares so much about community - there are literally dozens of scriptures about the need to have others around you:

- 1 Peter 4:8-11 ESV - "Above all, keep loving one another earnestly since love covers a multitude of sins. Show hospitality to one another without grumbling. As each has received a gift, use it to serve one another, as good stewards of God's varied grace: whoever speaks, as one who speaks oracles of God; whoever serves, as one who serves by the strength that God supplies—in order that in everything God may be glorified through Jesus Christ. To him belong glory and dominion forever and ever. Amen."

- Proverbs 27:17 NIV - "As iron sharpens iron, so one person sharpens another."

- Matthew 18:20 AMP - "For where two or three are gathered in My name [meeting together as My followers], I am there among them."

What communities are you a part of? How do those communities benefit from your Golden Spoon?

_____

_____

_____

_____

_____

_____

_____

Deeper and Deeper

As you're learning, this journey to finding purpose is really all about probing yourself in the deepest areas and pulling out your true values and learnings based on your life experiences. Guess what? The probing doesn't stop here.

Back in 2015, I (unofficially) officially launched Kendra Y. Hill Ministries. It was honestly never in my plans to do ministry publicly but we know that God is gonna get what He wants out of our lives one way or another. I hopped on Periscope because it was the new hot platform. I had never really live-streamed anywhere before so I had no idea if anyone would even watch me. My very first Periscope was about moonlighting - when you work your full-time job and build your business on the side. It was cool. To my surprise, nearly 200 people joined to hear me talk about how I left the San Antonio Spurs to start my own brand management firm. I remember getting off the scope thinking that was it. I would get on once a week and talk about business, but God had other plans.

The following week, I got on to talk about using your natural skills to make money and someone asked me about the most challenging time in my life. Before I knew it, I was sharing my story about being molested by my grandfather. After a tearful testimony about how I got out of the situation and how God used my Gammy's death to get me in church, I paused. Reading the comments on the screen, I noticed that multiple women were sharing their stories too. "He came to me while I was sleeping," @dsheare109 wrote. "It was my brother who raped me," @someone-saveme314 chimed in. @HolyGhostWriter777 added, "My mom didn't believe me but I knew that it happened. That's how I became a writer. I wanted to share women's stories."

I gained my composure as I heard the Lord tell me that I would win souls for Him by sharing my truth everywhere I went. God showed me that the impact would be great. That by helping others improve their lives, they would also help set others free. God showed me that I was called to live a transparent life online.

So I want you to think about this: how will the world be better off thanks to you having been on this earth?

_____

_____

_____

_____

_____

_____

_____

What comes to mind when you hear the word SUPERPOWER?

_____

_____

_____

_____

_____

_____

_____

_____

I realized at a young age that I was kind of different. From being able to see the ghost girl in my house as a toddler to dreaming about TWA Flight 800's crash the night before it happened, I was tapped into the supernatural at an early age. I hit my peak superpowers around the age of 26 when I fully submitted my life to God. As I worked through my process to purge the escort service-running, drug-dealing Kendra, God was unlocking the prophetic within me. I began to tap into my innate sense of knowing in even deeper ways and God started making my dreams make sense to me. The deeper I got into the word of God and the process of perfecting that He was taking me through, I was able to easily tap into the supernatural and see with understanding.

SUPERPOWER: noun \ ˈsü-pər-ˌpau̇(-ə)r \

excessive or superior power

All of my superpowers aren't extremely supernatural. Some of my "normal" ones are the ability to multi-task and juggle dozens of projects at once. Another one is my ability to be gracious under pressure and some would say that I have the patience of a saint (again, SOME would say because I personally don't think so lol). I want you to consider your own qualities, characteristics, and skills. What are your unique gifts and superpowers?

_____

_____

_____

_____

_____

_____

_____

When I look back over my life and consider the mountain tops (my most successful moments), I realize that I was both internally and externally at my best. We all know what that looks like, but do you realize that your best self has two parts? There's the best you that you put out to the world, but there's also the best things that are poured into you in order to be your best self. When I'm my best self to the world, I'm compassionate, loving, and kind, but honest. I have the knack for snatching your edges and reading you your rights in the most loving way possible. But I realized that presenting that person to the world comes from time behind closed doors where I feel loved, protected, and cared for. When I'm missing those components in my private life, the negative me shows up for the world. So, who have you been when you've been at your best? What contributes to the best self that the world receives?

_____

_____

_____

_____

_____

_____

_____

Reflecting on your Golden Spoon - if you were to use this one thing combined with the version of your best self you just described, who must you fearlessly become?

_____

_____

_____

_____

People approach me for all types of reasons. There are some people who think Kendra Y. Hill is synonymous with business or wealth. But honestly, the main thing people approach me about is spirituality and faith.

KENDRA: proper noun \ (ˈ)ken¦ drə \

the knowing woman; prophetess

Understanding what my name means has helped me in more ways than one. Not only has it given me clarity on one of my main gifts, but it has also given me permission to be wise at a young age. My mentees literally range from age 20 to 60 because people are seeking direction and they come to me to get it. What's something people always approach you about?

_____

_____

_____

_____

_____

_____

_____

Life comes at us fast, frfr. You can feel like you're in the right place, doing the right thing, and then BOOM! One thing happens and now you feel lost. Oftentimes, this is how purpose feels. You feel like you're in the right place doing the right things and then a detour sign comes up redirecting you to a neighborhood that you're unfamiliar with. Consider points in your life where you felt lost. What direction did God give you?

_____

_____

_____

_____

_____

_____

_____

_____

For me, God speaks like this in my wilderness:

> "Trust me. I am your God. I've got this. I am your Father. I haven't forgotten you. I am in control. Keep going. Greater is coming. I am with you, always."

Take rest knowing that He's got you in every area of your life, especially when it comes to seeking Him for your purpose. Believe it or not, we're so close to coming to a conclusive purpose statement, it ain't even funny! But before we get there, I need you to reflect.

Review your answers from this chapter. What are the 3 main things you learned about yourself?

1. _____

_____

2. _____

_____

3. _____

_____

My President is Black.
My Maybach, Too.

I want you to stop and congratulate yourself for making it this far! If you've followed the prompts and done all of the exercises as I laid them out, you've done a LOT of internal soul searching over the last few days. Let's segue into some external factors that can help shape your purpose.

When I was in the 4th grade, I moved to another part of town. Up until that point, I had lived in the suburbs of Converse which, back then, was the nice part of town. If you're from San Antonio, then think back to like 1998. This was before the major developments out at 281 and Loop 1604, so all of the upper-middle-class folks lived in Converse. Anyway, in 4th grade, I permanently moved to the east side of San Antonio, down the street from Dorie Miller Elementary School. My house sat on Robeson Avenue - the street before the railroad tracks.

Aside from the old school wooden walls that belonged in the '70s, the house also had slanted floors due to foundation issues. When you would stand in the den, you had to bend one knee so you could keep your balance. Speaking of the den, it was actually an addition to the original structure, as was the master bedroom. The 3 bedroom, 1 bathroom, 1,280 sq. foot house was home to 5 people. We didn't have central air conditioning or heat. Instead, we had two window units that ran in the summer and three gas stoves that had to be hand-lit with a match that heated the house in the winter. And did I mention the railroad tracks? Our house was so close to the train tracks that when a freight train passed through our neghborhood, the whole house shook.

We dealt with our fair share of "hood disease." From seeing the make-shift altars filled with teddy bears, candles, and empty Hennessy bottles for loved ones who were murdered in the street to hearing gunshots all night, growing up on the east side was challenging. I saw a homeless man shooting heroin for the first time on a street by my house when I was 12. My mom and I were driving to the library one day so I could do some research when a drive-by shooting popped off right in front of us. Every other week, kids got murdered at the basketball court at the end of our street.

Worse than the crime and violence in my neighborhood were the roaches. If you know anything about roaches in Texas, then you know that they're huge AND they fly. We had roaches in our house almost every single night. It didn't matter how clean the house was, you could almost bank on a roach crawling in through one of the holes or crevices in the house. BUT, there was something worse than the roaches.

During the summer months, 311 was plagued with tarantulas. Big, hairy, and scary tarantulas would enter the house through the mailslot by the front door. My stepdad used to send me outside at night to take the trash out and I would literally put on boots and run through the yard for fear of a creepy, crawly spider running across my foot. It was hard to have hope for a better life growing up in those conditions.

Entered my pastor's wife, Rev. Linda Thompson. Even though she was indeed an ordained reverend, it would be years before she was properly recognized as the co-pastor of Holy Nation Baptist Church. Anyway, I met Rev. Linda shortly after Gammy died. I think about that often. If Gammy wouldn't have died, I wouldn't have ever gone to church. Up until her death, I had only been to church a handful of times; a couple of funerals for elder family members and a summer vacation bible school.

I was struggling to cope with Gammy's death so Lillie Mae thought it would be good for me to start attending youth bible study at Holy Nation. When I entered the church, we stepped into a sanctuary full of energetic, rambunctious children. Even though I was only 8 years old, I was really mature for my age. I got nervous. I already didn't really fit in at school (I was fat and too smart for my own good), so I was already prepared to be bullied at this church, too.

I sat on the front row as the pastor led the congregation in opening prayer. As all of the adults left the sanctuary to have their study in smaller meeting rooms, the children all moved over to the side of the room that I was sitting on. Two other little girls sat on the front row next to me. They silently gawked at the giant white family bible that was resting on my lap. I didn't have a personal bible, but I knew that if I was going to a bible study, I had to have a holy book. I had taken the family bible off the credenza at the house. It was dusty and the white cover was starting to turn yellow, but it was what I had.

Rev. Linda didn't bat an eyelash. She was a middle school choir teacher who didn't play and these kids already knew it. They quietly rose from their seats to recite the books of the bible from memory. I didn't even know what a Genesis or a Revelation was, so I sat with my back stiff as a board, looking directly at Rev. Linda who was sitting in a chair right in front of me. Once the children finished saying all 66 books of the bible, they sat down and we started our lesson.

As Rev. Linda called out the scriptures for that night's lesson, the older kids began flipping through the pages of their appropriately-sized bibles to find the text. They were skimming and flipping so fast that you could hear pages nearly tearing as they raced to be the first to find the readings. I was a total novice but Rev. Linda was patient with me. "Kendra, can you read Genesis 12 beginning with the first verse?" She leaned forward and helped me locate the text. Some of the kids snickered and laughed. I didn't know if it was because I had this textbook-sized bible on my lap or because I couldn't find the very first book of the bible. Hell, they may have been laughing because I was fluffy. Regardless, I cleared my throat and began to read the scripture. "Now the Lord had said unto Abram, Get thee out of thy country, and from thy kindred, and from thy father's house, unto a land that I will shew thee…"

I read with such clarity and diction that the whole room fell dead. It was so quiet, you could hear the mockingbirds chirping outside. One of the older kids was the first to break the silence. "Wow!" Gabrielle remarked. Some of the other kids started clapping and cheering for me. Rev. Linda looked at me with a knowing smile and continued to teach.

After bible study was over and the whole church had prayed out and been dismissed, Rev. Linda put her arm around my shoulders and said, "Kendra, you are a brilliant little girl. I see so much of myself in you." She walked me over to Lillie Mae who was beaming from ear to ear. "Sis. Lillie, you have yourself a very special granddaughter." Lillie went on to tell Rev. Linda about my scholastic achievements as we walked outside to the parking lot.

Over the next 10+ years, Rev. Linda took me under her wing and mentored me. She showed me so many things that I wouldn't have had the opportunity to experience as an east side kid who had survived childhood rape. She took me to the cultural arts center to see the Alvin Ailey dancers as I was a star liturgical dancer at Holy Nation. We went to every gospel concert that came to town and when an African dance teacher started at her school, she picked me up from W. W. White Elementary School so I could participate with the older kids on her campus.

It wasn't all tulips and roses, though. Rev. Linda chastised me harshly - often. She would fuss at me before church if my bra or foundational garments were out of place. Once I reached junior high, she had access to me every single day. Even though she was the choir director at S.J. Davis Middle School, she ran that building. If I was a little ripe after P.E., she would call me to the auditorium where she held her class and fuss at me while I put on the deodorant she kept in her drawer.

But more than anything, Rev. Linda gave me hope. She used to write me these little notes and letters in her spare time. They were like her way of imparting wisdom to me when she didn't have the opportunity to spend time with me. Her notes ranged from words of encouragement to expressions of love. Sometimes she would talk about what she and

Pastor were up to. Sometimes she would update me on her own educational journey as she was working on her second master's in the hopes of getting her doctorate. She always signed her notes as "Rev. Mama" - because she was. She didn't have any natural children of her own, but she loved me like I was hers and I needed the extra attention and push.

One day, she presented her note in a white letter-sized envelope. It was plush and thick like it had multiple pages. I couldn't wait to get home after school to see what she had written. Once I reached my bedroom, I tore open the envelope as if my life depended on it. There were four pages of typed text and a fifth page that had some kind of computer graphic on it. I waited to check out the last page because I knew Rev. Linda had planned her presentation. The written letter was a lengthy-expression of her pride in me. She told me that I could do anything. She told me that I could BE anything. She explained that she wanted to be a lawyer as a child, but her mom made her go to school to be a teacher. She didn't want that for me. Rev. Linda wanted me to be whatever I wanted to be. "You could even be the first African-American female President of the United States of America," she wrote. I looked at the last page with the picture on it and realized that it was the seal of the President. She had calculated the year that I would be eligible to run for president by age and the first year I could actually be elected (an election year). They were 2022 and 2024, respectively.

SN: It's crazy looking at this now as it's currently 2022 when I'm writing this book. God also told me back in 2020 that my word for 2022 was "mine" and that everything that was meant for me would come to me. Obviously, I'm not planning to run for President, but how crazy is it that she had that much foresight and that we're currently in the era where I could have been running for office. Spicy!

From that moment on, I really believed that I could do and be absolutely anything. Rev. Linda was an intelligent, sharp-witted, and influential community leader. If she believed in me, then I knew that I must have been special.

It goes without saying that mentors are important. I know I talk about mentorship a lot, but I know how those relationships literally saved my life on top of making me a better businesswoman. I've learned that you don't have enough time in your lifetime to learn everything you need to know to be wildly successful. There comes a point where you can't do it on your own anymore. When I was starting Kendra, Scale My Business, my mentor Silas really led me to transition my old clients into my new structure as well as gain new clients quickly. His advice is one of the main reasons I became a multi-million dollar business in less than 2 years.

The greatest thing that mentorship has done for me is expand my mind to believe the impossible. It didn't make sense for Rev. Linda to work so hard to convince me - a girl who had been sexually assaulted for years and was now living in poverty - that I could be anything, even the President of the United States. But there's no doubt in my mind that those words and that push gave me the courage to pursue my dreams with full confidence.

I want you to get your own mentors in mind. Think about the people who have helped mold you into the person you are today. What are some things that they have said to you about you that stuck with you?

_____

_____

_____

_____

_____

_____

_____

_____

Let's take it a step further. What are some prophetic words that you've received in your life about your future? These could have come through journaling and time with God, from viewing a message online or from an actual prophet. What is God saying about your future? I want you to dig deep and reflect because we usually forget these things when life gets tough. This space will serve as a reminder that God has a plan for you and He's still going to do exactly what He said.

_____

_____

_____

_____

_____

_____

_____

09 I Can Show You the World

We all LOVE a good vacation. Shoot, at this point, I'll take a mediocre business trip. It's no secret that travel is a great way to shift your perception, ignite creativity, and inspire even the savviest global citizen. But have you ever considered how travel helps you on your journey to finding purpose?

Surprisingly, the story I'm about to tell you isn't about the trip itself as much as it is about the revelation that I got while traveling. My man and I decided to start working on our own personal film projects outside of work. Nixon was the star of a viral Christian web series and I was on the heels of wrapping a television show that I was producing. We both had a real passion for film and television, but we knew it was time to start working on our own things. His was a global travel show focused on culture through a Christian lens while mine was a show about going to various U.S. cities and staying awake for 24 hours with no hotel (I might revive the idea soon, so don't be trying to take my intellectual property lol).

My first city was New York - as the city that doesn't sleep, it should be easy to be up all night. We had a great time. Between shopping at Macy's Herald Square, crying over the cheesecake at Junior's, and hunting for a public restroom (there aren't any, btw), we had a blast. We ended the morning at Battery Park watching the sunrise over Lady Liberty. We had to drive to Boston for a conference the next day, so we headed to a hotel to get some much-needed rest.

The next afternoon we got on the road for our 3.5-hour drive to Beantown. In typical "us" fashion, we made a million stops. We're the couple that can turn a 4-hour drive into an 8-hour adventure between stopping for Starbucks and checking out local attractions. Leaving our last Starbucks of the trip, I situated myself in the car to get ready for the final hour on the road. We started talking about my life and all of the things I've experienced, both good and bad. On that stretch of road, I had an epiphany: my life was really a living epistle. I had seen and done so much that it was clear that I needed to pray about how God wanted me to share my story. Through my tear-stained eyes, I saw the exit for our hotel and heard my man say, "This is totally in alignment with your purpose" as he grabbed my hand.

That trip was the start of a series of conversations that led to a MAJOR discovery that completely rocked my world. Although it wasn't The Big Apple that unearthed this revelation, it WAS the fact that I was away from home and experiencing a new environment. Often times when we feel stuck or lost and in need of some direction, traveling is our compass and guide.

Think about a trip you've taken or a place you've lived where you felt like your best self. Maybe you backpacked through Thailand or visited the Midwest for the first time. Perhaps it's a place where you lived. Whatever it is, get that trip in your mind as you answer these questions.

Where did you go? Did you live there or visit?

_____

_____

_____

_____

_____

_____

_____

_____

What made it so special to you?

_____

_____

_____

_____

_____

_____

_____

What are some things you learned?

_____

_____

_____

_____

_____

_____

_____

What did you learn about yourself? If you don't know, take a moment and think about the trip. Remember the smells, the sounds, the food. What did you do? Were there any moments that just felt blissful? What made it that way?

_____

_____

_____

_____

_____

_____

_____

_____

Can I? Baby?

Now, I can hear some of you "awwing" to the story I told about my man. He is by FAR the natural key to the best me. When I think about being my best self, memories with him come to mind. He makes me feel protected, loved, and cared for in so many ways. But he also holds up the mirror and calls me to the carpet.

Back in 2019 when I was at the peak of frustration with my purpose, I shared my concerns with him. Nixon is always a listening ear, but he's also not afraid to tell me that my crap stinks. Honestly, he's exactly what I need because let's be honest - I would run over a man like Stedman. One morning I called him on Facetime to whine and cry about the lack of motivation I had. The convo went a little something like this:

>   Nixon: Good morning, sweaty! (don't ask lol)
>
>   Me: It's not a good morning *pouting*
>
>   Nixon: Oh no, babe! What's wrong?
>
>   Me: I just don't feel motivated to do anything. I don't feel like I have a purpose.
>
>   Nixon: Sure you do. It's to be with me.
>
>   Me: *stares blankly at the screen in disbelief*

I just knew this man wasn't telling me that my life's purpose was to be with him! I hung up the phone after a few dry pleasantries and went back to sleep. I felt so sad and so empty. I prayed really hard and went on about my day.

The next morning, my spiritual little sister Makiyah called me with a word. She shared that God had a plan for me beyond my marriage. That everything I had experienced in my life would play a part in my purpose. That my purpose was great because I was so special to God. Though these words should have given me peace, I felt like I was listening to the teacher on Charlie Brown, "Whomp whomp whomp." What should have given me peace really just annoyed me, but it didn't stop there.

The very next morning, I woke up to a text from Nixon:

"Good morning, sweaty! I hope you slept well. God gave me a message to give to you. Give me five minutes and I'll text it."

So not only was God sending voice notes through Makiyah, but now he was sending telegrams through Nixon *insert eyeroll here*. I was over it. The words that followed really had me hemmed up:

"Your time is coming. You just have to be patient. God has not forgotten anything He has promised you. You're doing all of the preparation right now, so when the flood that you're expecting hits, you will be prepared and you don't have to scramble. It's another level of God testing your faith. You've heard God about going back into consulting but you have to stop being frustrated. You're trying to fulfill your purpose your way - God is trying to break that."

As irritated as I was, I knew I had to pray. I spent the next few weeks in prayer and prayed myself all the way into exile (but I digress).

The real point is that God puts people in our lives (romantic, familial, and platonic relationships) to help us on our journey. Oftentimes, we want to ignore them because we feel like they're too close or that they're speaking to us from a selfish place. Don't get it twisted - some people do. You have to evaluate what they're saying and you can really only do that in prayer. Though I didn't want to hear what Makiyah or Nixon were saying, they were both right. God DID have a big plan for me. My purpose WAS found through my experiences. God WAS trying to prepare me for the flood. But it took me a whole period of exile to finally surrender and submit.

I want you to consider your own circle. Do you have friends, family members, or a significant other who is speaking into your life? Who are the trusted voices in your life?

_____

_____

_____

_____

_____

_____

_____

What are some of the uncomfortable things they have said that you may need to deeply consider and pray about?

_____

_____

_____

_____

_____

_____

_____

Until the Pain is Gone

Since we're talking about trusted voices, let me tell you about your boy Nixon. If I ever had any doubts in mind that he was my person, this one particular incident washed them all away. (trigger warning: sexual abuse).

It was September 24, 2017, when Nixon and I were celebrating our anniversary in Dallas. We had a great weekend planned including all of our favorite things: going to the movies, dining in the best restaurants the city had to offer and working. Yes, working. We're both workaholics and we honestly spend so much of our time together working on our projects and building our businesses.

Anyway, as we returned to our hotel from watching *Girls Trip*, Nixon started asking me questions about my childhood. We had been together for a few years at this point, but my family dynamic and adolescence had pretty much been an enigma. We exited the elevator and started walking down the hallway to our room. Nixon was looking for the room key while I was looking for an appropriate photo of my mother that I could show him. Once we entered the room, he grabbed my phone and said, "Wow! You and your mom look so much alike. Almost like sisters. That's wild." We spent the rest of the evening chatting about my family and what it was like growing up in San Antonio.

The conversation made me think back to a dream I had the month before. In the dream, I was flipping through a filing cabinet looking for my name. Once I found my manila folder, I opened it to review the files. There were lots of different things in the folder; photos, press clippings, documents, etc. I placed the folder on top of the filing cabinet when I got to my birth certificate. On the line marked "mother" was my mom's name: MARINA HILL. On the line marked "father", there was a blurred name but I knew it wasn't Tim. I woke up and started trying to make sense of what I had seen in my sleep.

Tim McKinnon was my father - or so I thought. According to my mom, she and Tim were high school sweethearts. He was her first and she got pregnant the first time they had sex - they were both 16 years old. Tim was freaked out about having a kid, so he ended up joining the military shortly after I was born. Throughout my childhood, I never really thought too much about the fact that I didn't have a dad. Shoot, most of my friends didn't have one either, so I never felt out of place.

The dream about my birth certificate bothered me, but I had put it to the back of my mind until Nixon brought up the gaps in my family history. Shortly after our anniversary celebration, I went back home and spent some time thinking about Tim. In 2008 when I was about to turn 21, I had asked my mom about the details concerning him. I was working on Capitol Hill and I had access to all types of top-secret information. I knew that if I ever wanted to find my dad, that was the time. My mom told me that Tim McKinnon was adopted into a family that lived in a neighboring community. He was Puerto Rican and Black, his birthday was June 14th and his adopted dad was a man named Gary.

Armed with this information, I went back to my desk in Congressman Farr's office and began my search. In less than 5 minutes, I found a phone number that was linked to a Gary McKinnon in Converse, Texas. I quickly stepped out into the hallway and dialed the 210 phone number. An elderly man answered the phone and the conversation went a little something like this:

Maybe Gary: Hello?

Me: Hi, may I please speak to Tim?

Maybe Gary: (aggressively) Who is THIS???

Me: Well, it's kind of a long story, but I think that Tim is my father.

click

Old man Gary hung up in my face. And mans was on a landline, so he slammed the phone down with the satisfaction of the dude who told Mary 'nem that there was no room in the inn. I was kind of upset, but I understood where he was coming from. How would I have reacted? Probably worse, TBH. I went back to my desk so I could try to find another number to reach Tim. No sooner than I reached my office, my phone rang with that same 210 number. "Call this number," old man Gary mumbled. And with that, he rattled off 10 digits and slammed the phone down again.

I walked down the hallway to call the mysterious 512 number. Well, at least I knew that Tim lived in Austin. As the phone rang, my hands began to shake. I was super nervous to hear the voice of my father. Imagine my surprise when a woman cooed, "Hello?" on the other end of the phone. It must've taken me a moment to respond because the soft-spoken woman repeated herself with a bit of an attitude. "Hello?!?" Somehow I gained my composure and asked to speak to Tim. She really found her voice then. "WHO is THIS??!?" Realizing that this was probably his wife thinking I was the "other woman," I quickly answered. "It's kind of a long story, but I believe that Tim is my biological father. I would be his oldest child. My name is Kendra." The relief that his wife felt radiated through the phone and permeated my ears. "Oh my goodness! Your father told me all about you. He hasn't seen you since you were a baby. Oh, he's an amazing man and he's gonna be so glad to hear from you!" she ranted. After a 10-minute conversation about the super amazing Tim, Mrs. McKinnon took down my phone number and promised that she would have her husband call me.

Sure enough, around 7:00 pm, my phone rang with another 512 phone number and I knew that it was him. I was nervous to talk to my father, but I was excited to finally learn about the other side of my family. Tim sounded excited too, which was a great feeling. I was glad to know that he had been thinking about me all of these years. I quickly let him know that I didn't want any money and my mom wasn't mad at him - I just wanted to learn more about my genetics and the father I never knew. After a 4-hour conversation, we agreed to meet at Christmas when I was back in the area.

I called my mom to share the news, but she wasn't as excited as I was. Her sober temperament was a blow to my own joy, but with good reason.

I learned that Tim was a detective in Leander, Texas which was less than 2 hours away from San Antonio. My mom felt that if Tim wanted to know me and had been thinking about me as much as he said he had, surely he would've been able to find me. Call me naive, but I believed Tim. He had other children and a whole wife, plus he was a forensic detective so he was always sleep-deprived. I wasn't worried.

Chile. Mama knows best because this negro sent me this email 2 days later:

> Hello,
>
> I got both of your e-mails. I also received your voice message. I don't want you to think that I don't want to talk with you. I'm just at a loss for words. I'm looking for the right words to say. The night we talked I was on an infant death investigation as you can imagine those are tough investigations to investigate. And not trying to make excuses but a majority of the time I'm very busy at work and I have so much on my plate that I forget to do things. Your contacting me is still a big shock for me as well as my wife. Things have been on edge with her. I'm good at helping others with their needs but when it comes to my own that's another story. To make a long story short I just don't know how to go about all of this.
>
> To be totally honest I never thought that I would ever meet you. On the inside, I am embarrassed about the whole situation, and to add to it Genesis (my other daughter) and I just established a relationship as well. Me and her mother had a bad break up and some other things happen as well so I just basically paid child support over the years. She is very upset because she thinks I lied to her and her mother. I'm just not good at the father thing I guess. And this is terrible timing too. I will be in Atlanta over Christmas. I should have let you know sooner. We are going to my wife's cousin's wedding. The night I talked to you it was the farthest thing from my mind. I just don't have room for you in my life.
>
> Goodbye for now.
>
> Timothy

Flash forward to 2017 and I was sitting in my house crying while I re-read the email that Tim had sent so many years ago. Seeing the words, "I. JUST. DON'T. HAVE. ROOM. FOR. YOU. IN. MY. LIFE." was crushing my heart all over again. I cried myself to sleep that night.

About a week or so later, I started to experience debilitating back pain that left me bedridden. During this time, everyone on my prayer team started having mild symptoms of my sickness, too. Some had headaches while others felt back pain. A couple of them even had the nausea and inflammation I was experiencing. I knew it was spiritual warfare, but I couldn't pinpoint why. One night after struggling to fall asleep, I had a dream that set everything off again. Much like the dream I had a few weeks back, God was trying to show me that Tim wasn't my father.

After I finally got off of what felt like my deathbed, I hit up my then-best friend Janine to chat about my suspicions. I told her that I wanted to drive to Austin to DNA test Tim. I needed to know the truth and being a true ride or die, I knew she would be down for the trip. We planned to go see Timmy in 4 days.

Well, anyone who knows me knows that I don't do well with holding onto information that feels contentious, so the next evening, my mom and I had a little come to Jesus chat. She had just walked in from work but I knew I couldn't hold my peace any longer. As she walked into the kitchen, I bombarded her with a million questions:

- "Why aren't there more photos of me as a child?"

- "Are you really my mom?"

- "Who is my dad?"

- "My birth certificate says it was issued in March of 1988, but I was born on October 24, 1987. Something is suspicious."

My mom looked over at me from the kitchen sink and kinda rolled her eyes. "Why would you ask me all of this? Of course, I'm your mom. And yes, you were born on October 24th. And I told you that Tim was your dad." I just couldn't hold it any longer. "Mom, I had a dream." My mom snapped her neck around toward me so fast that she should've gotten whiplash. Everybody in my life knows that if I have a dream, you can bet your life on it. She slowly walked across the kitchen and joined me at the dining room table. I recanted the dream about my birth certificate and the blurred name without pausing to take a breath.

"Who is my father?" I calmly asked. At this point, I just wanted the truth. I was a big girl; I could take it. "WHO is my father, mom?" My mom put her head down and tears started to form in her eyes. "Mom. Please just tell me. Who is my father?" The intensity grew rapidly as I kept asking the same question over and over. Suddenly, my mom started to sob loudly. It was as if her tears broke the dam and I heard the voice of the Lord so clearly say,

"Charles."

"Is it Charles???" I asked in disbelief. My mom looked at me with pain in her eyes as if she too had just heard God say that devilish man's name. "If it's not Tim, then it must be. Charles was raping me around that time." Her sobbing grew louder and louder. The rage that raced through my body was moving faster than Jeff Gordon in a NASCAR race. "Oh my God! This makes so much sense," she exclaimed. The more I waited on her to confirm what the Holy Spirit had already said, the angrier I became. "Charles had invited Tim over to the house and basically encouraged us to have sex around the time I got pregnant with you. Charles also had all of my pregnancy symptoms and he's the one who made me go get tested." As her thoughts trailed off, my patience did too. I jumped up and flipped the dining room table over as I stormed off to my room. I was heated. Here I was 10 days away from turning 30 and I was just now finding out that my grandfather (who raped me repeatedly as a child) was also my father.

It was a lot to process but I was honestly too hurt to even think about it all. I was a product of incest. My grandfather was my father. My mother was my sister (just like Nixon had suggested). I was devastated. Lying across my bed, I googled "scriptures about incest". I may have been angry, but I wasn't stupid. I needed to know what God was saying about all of this. The first scripture that came up was Leviticus 18:6-18 which outlined all of the various relationships that would be considered incest. It wasn't just blood relationships; the scripture covered in-laws and some more. None of that applied to me because it was a CLEAR delineation that this was indeed incest. The next sampling of scripture was found in chapter 20 of Leviticus which outlined the consequences of the person who committed incest. Still not helpful. I threw my bible across the room out of frustration. I didn't know who to call or what to do, but the longer I sat in my room, the angrier I became. How could God do this to me? How could He let this happen to me? And my mom - had she known all along and was just too ashamed to say anything? How could they do this to me?

My frustration quickly snowballed into rebellion. If this is how God was going to treat me, then I wasn't going to speak to Him. I was probably cursed anyway, so what was the point? I laid on my back and stared at the ceiling. The low moonlight dancing behind the trees and shining through my blinds was the only light in the room. My heart and soul felt just as dark as my former sanctuary.

I turned on my side to prepare myself for bed. Maybe I could sleep it all off and wake up refreshed. I closed my eyes and nestled under the covers for some well-deserved rest when I heard a noise. It started as a single whisper…"Kendra." The voice was unfamiliar and quite distant. I almost thought it was my mom trying to come in and chat about my discovery, but then the voice multiplied. "Kendra. Kendra. Kendraaaaaa," the voices started calling out. I opened my eyes and sat straight up in the bed. Reaching over to turn on the lamp by my nightstand, I looked around to see who was up in here playing with me. I was tired and emotionally worn out. I really just wanted to take my tail to bed and try again tomorrow. I turned off the light, laid back down, and closed my eyes again only to hear the voices even louder than before. "KENDRA! KENDRA! KENDRA!" The sound was almost that of a tribal chant. I realized that I was being tormented.

TORMENT: noun \ tȯr-ˈment \

to cause severe usually persistent or recurrent distress of body or mind

I hadn't dealt with a tormenting spirit in a very long time - I usually only faced them when praying for other people at the altar. Tormenting spirits take advantage of an open door (a crevice, space, or room where sin has entered the chat). At that moment, I thought that incest was the sin that created a portal for torment, but hindsight being 20/20, it was my reaction to the news that created an opening. SMH. I wish I would have realized it then. The bible is clear that we are to "be angry, sin not" (Ephesians 4:26). We all experience emotions in life, but it's whether or not we act on the emotion that makes the difference. You can literally put any emotion in that scripture - Be happy, sin not. Be frustrated, sin not. Be sad, sin not. - and the sentiment applies. I acted in sin by flipping over the table, throwing my bible, and totally disregarding God in an act of rebellion.

The torment didn't stop at the whispers. For three days, I didn't get one minute of sleep. As soon as I would get to the edge of sleep, SOME-THING would happen. First, it was the whispers. Then I started hearing these voices calling me names. "B****. Slut. Whore." I could take the name-calling, but I almost fully lost it when the balloons started popping. I would hear the sound of helium filling balloons and then popping. We were about a week away from my 30th birthday at this point and the de-mons were literally bursting my bubble.

I couldn't take it anymore. Aside from the torment, the lack of sleep was driving me insane. My mom and I hadn't spoken since I flipped the table like Jesus in the temple. I just couldn't formulate anything nice to say. It wasn't fair because she was just as much of a victim as I was. I had spent some time sharing the story with some very close friends and every time I spoke to someone about it, I cried. Every conversation was helping me purge the pain, but I still didn't feel any relief.

That third night was the worst. I had decided to kill myself. I couldn't find any relief in this life, but I knew that I would find relief on the other side.

My mom was at work and though it pained me to think of how she would find me upon her return home, I had to be selfish. I needed to get free from this pain. I went to the closet and opened up the safe I had hidden in the back. My mom didn't even know there was a safe there, let alone that I had a gun. I grabbed the Beretta, made sure my phone was on silent, and went into the bathroom. I never thought I would get to this point, but here I was - Prophetess Kendra, sitting on the bathroom floor preparing to commit suicide.

As my hot and unmanageable tears slammed into the tiled floor, my whole life flashed before my eyes. I still had very vivid memories of Charles' violent rapings. His appetite was insatiable and he sodomized me often - he wanted everything. I went back to my childhood bedroom decked out in every Little Mermaid decor item my mom could find. I had curtains, sheets, a comforter, a night light, and a side table lamp that glowed in the dark. The retrospection had been eclipsed by the facts - this demon was my father. My freakin' father!

I lifted the 9mm to my head and prepare to end it all. My shallow chest breathing turned into deep diaphragmatic breaths that rattled my lungs. I didn't know if I was having an anxiety attack or if I was just hyperventilating, but I couldn't control the cadence of my breaths. Suddenly, I heard the distinct sound of an iPhone ringing. The cheerful notes echoed from my bedroom into the tiny acoustic reflecting bathroom. How was my phone ringing? I ALWAYS kept it on silent and I even double-checked it before I committed to my task at hand. Begrudgingly, I got up to find out what was happening.

I picked up the phone to see that Janine was calling me. She was the first person I called three days before to share my life-changing news. I reluctantly answered the phone. "Hello?" I asked sadly. "I don't know what's going on with you right now but God just told me to sit on the phone with you in silence." At that moment, I broke and my face melted into a puddle of uncontrollable tears. Janine's male best friend had just murdered himself in front of her at her house a couple of years before. My best friend was just getting over the impact that incident had on her. I couldn't kill myself with her on the phone and subject her to another traumatic episode. I don't know if it was the physical exhaustion or the emotional weight, but I passed out and immediately fell asleep.

Of course, God spoke to me in my sleep. I was too stubborn to surrender to Him while I was awake. In the dream, I was in a big house that had multiple floors. I was sleeping in the hallway by a grand staircase when I woke up to use the bathroom. Tipping around the house to not disturb anyone, I saw my Apostle and Nixon having a conversation in the living room. They appeared to be happy and enjoying each other's company. Instead of heading to the bathroom, I walked directly to the kitchen and opened the refrigerator. Then I did the unthinkable: I pooped inside the refrigerator. After pulling up my pajamas, I went to look around and see if anyone saw me. I knew it wasn't the right thing to do, but it's what felt right. After surveying the first floor for any witnesses, I went back to the kitchen and opened the refrigerator to find that my fecal matter had turned into nachos. Then I heard the voice of the Lord. "Clean everything out. Bleach it all or everything will be contaminated." So I followed the instructions I was given and emptied the fridge and bleached every surface inside. When I turned back to the refrigerator, there was water, fruits, and vegetables inside. I woke up.

When I opened my natural eyes, I was a bit dazed and confused. I hadn't slept the whole night, but it was close to the time my mom would be coming home. I ran to the bathroom to grab my firearm and secure it before she could see the near-crime scene. After I locked up the safe, I sat on the side of my bed to collect my thoughts. I couldn't make sense of pooping in the refrigerator, so I asked God to help me. His voice was just as clear as it was in the dream. "I'm trying to cleanse you of this pain and you're trying to preserve the purge. This is counterproductive. My plan is for you to be free." How I still had liquid in my tear ducts, I'm not sure, but the water flowed freely onto my pillow. I repented and I knew what I had to do.

I ended up calling my prayer circle and letting them know that it was time for a fast. Taking a cue from the dream, we would only have water, fruits, and vegetables for the next 7 days. We'd end at 12:01 am on October 24th - my 30th birthday.

Writing this book is the first time I have shared this story en masse. I even debated about removing It. What would people think about me after they heard my truth? How would this impact the way I was perceived online? The stigma around being a product of incest almost made me erase what may be the most powerful chapter in this entire text. "People are going to immediately label me as ugly or stupid," I thought to myself. But what I quickly realized is that each of our life's experiences - especially, the bad ones - are for someone else. Everything that we go through is meant to not only make us stronger but also to serve as a witness to what God can do when we let Him handle it.

We talked about pain a while back, but this time, we need to dig into the unknown things. Unless you have knowledge of every moment of your life from conception until now, it's quite possible that you also have some hidden things lurking. It may not be incest, but it could be a secret that your family has been keeping from you. Maybe you were molested as a child, but you don't remember it, or your brain has blocked it from you as a form of protection. There could even be conversations and word curses that have been spoken over you by people you know and love. Whatever it is, let's deal with it.

My purpose really got accelerated when this hidden thing was revealed to me and healed IN me. Spiritually, there is warfare happening all around us. What a lot of us don't realize is that the same way there are laws on earth, there are laws in the realm of the spirit. If the enemy and his camp have been granted permission to act in a way and they are following the rules, they can keep holding you hostage until they act of character or God destroys the bondage. 2 Chronicles 7:14 NIV says, "If my people, who are called by my name, will humble themselves and pray and seek my face and turn from their wicked ways, then I will hear from heaven, and I will forgive their sin and will heal their land." The "land" here isn't just the geographical region; it also means the composition of people. God desires to heal YOU. But you have to pray, seek His face, and repent to get there.

I want you to take a moment to pray. In fact, I want you to pray for 3 consecutive days. If you can fast from food, then add that too. I know that may seem like a long time, but if you can get into an intimate space with God for a decent period of time, He can reveal a lot to you. He actually desires to share secrets with you when you commune with Him. While you're praying (or immediately after), I want you to take some notes on anything that comes up. I mean, ANYTHING. If God shows you numbers, colors, street signs, faces - anything - I want you to make a note of it. Throughout the rest of this journey, keep praying on anything that is revealed to you.

_____

_____

_____

_____

_____

_____

_____

_____

_____

_____

_____

_____

_____

_____

_____

_____

12

I Don't Wanna Leave.
But I Gotta Go Right Now.

This whole discussion about people speaking into your life reminds me of when I was working for the San Antonio Spurs. I had finally fully settled back in San Antonio after living in DC for 5 years. I was back at my home church serving in a variety of capacities while working my full-time job at the basketball arena. Though I enjoyed most of the work I did, I felt way out of alignment.

ALIGN: intransitive verb \ ə-'līn \

to be in or come into precise adjustment or correct relative position

I was out of place. I had decided that I was going to run for a city council seat (after being convinced by some influential folks who were setting me up to fail). The incumbent for my home district was quietly a disgrace and no one of any real merit would run against her. As a recent graduate of the illustrious Howard University with a degree in political science, I felt more than ready to tackle the beast (whew - I was overzealous). Beyond thinking I knew everything about politics, my desire really was to help people in my community. God had a plan for me.

The day that my city council application was due, I sat at my desk in the AT&T Center feeling very antsy. For some reason, I had so much anxiety about something I had been planning on doing for months. At 23, I would have been the youngest person to have ever been elected to the city council had I won. I sat in my car during lunch debating on what to do when I heard God's voice so clearly tell me to take my campaign slogan of "I Am San Antonio" and turn it into a business. IASA Consulting Group was born.

Around this time, I was called into my THEN Pastor's office for a meeting. I wasn't sure what it was about this time as I had been called in for several things over the many years I served there (mostly to be questioned about why I did or didn't do something or how I needed to improve a system that was already working, but I digress).

In this instance, I had been called in to discuss my own future. After explaining that I had just filled out my paperwork to start my business and I ultimately planned on going into my own business full-time, the Pastor formed his fingers together under his chin, almost like a church steeple. He peered at me over his no-line bifocals and said, "You need to stick it out at the Spurs and make this your career. This little business you have is just a hobby. It's not worth pursuing."

I was crushed. He and his wife were SUPER important in my life so to hear them say that my dream was a hobby nearly destroyed me. I honestly don't remember what happened next, but somehow I ended up in my car driving back to the AT&T Center for a Spurs game, crying all the way there.

Based on that advice, I stayed at the Spurs for about 5 months while moonlighting at IASA, but I didn't have peace, Between God's voice calling me to go dive into my business full-time and the bureaucracy and red tape I experienced working for the NBA, I knew it was time to go. I was in our normal Monday morning meeting where we go over the sales goals for the week. While everyone was excitedly sharing their plans to hit their sales, I was doodling on the side of my agenda. My mind hadn't been there for a while but I just didn't have the faith to leave with no real plan. As the meeting adjourned, I walked to the administrative assistant's desk and asked for a box. She brought a file box to my desk and I started packing it up. It took me about 2 hours, but I had packed my office, written my exit memo and letter of resignation, and was headed out the door.

Two days later, I got my first client at IASA Consulting Group. A church that wanted me to build them a website and optimize their Facebook offered me $10K to complete the work by the end of the month. As much as the conversation with my Pastor and his wife hurt me emotionally, it helped me find my footing. That one conversation turned my "hobby" into a brand management business with 3 offices, 18 employees, and millions of dollars (THAT hobby turned into a career as a stylist that generated 6-figures annually and THAT hobby turned into a business that has made over $6M in 2 years). My alignment had been off for half a year and I didn't realize it.

When we're discussing alignment here, we're talking about it in a spiritual sense. It means that you are aligned with what you are here to do during different seasons of your life. When you are spiritually aligned, you are able to become mentally and physically aligned with your purpose as well.

Think about your car. When your alignment is off, even just on one side, the whole vehicle will veer off on its own. You have to work a lot harder to get where you are going and keep the vehicle in the right direction. When your car is in perfect alignment, you can actually take your hands off the steering wheel and it will drive in a straight line. Becoming spiritually aligned is a lot like taking your car to the mechanic to get an adjustment.

Aside from holding on to old things way too long (i.e. me at the Spurs), being too future-focused can cause us to get out of alignment as well. It's a very normal (human) response to feel anxious about things, but we have to make peace with our pace. For a lot of people, being at peace with wherever they are in their process is a really tough feat. It's me; I'm people lol. It's easy to spend time comparing ourselves to the people around us, especially in a world where we're so heavily focused on social media. We start to feel like we're behind because it looks like everyone else is so far ahead. But at one point or another, you have to put on your blinders and focus on running your own individual race. You will get to where you're going when you're MEANT to get there and we're all called to do different things at different times to ultimately fulfill our purpose. This is what it means to be in alignment with God's plan!

Have you ever worked a job that felt right for a while, and suddenly one day you found yourself bored, or super anxious to have to go in? Maybe you just felt unsatisfied all of a sudden. That's a good cue to leave! You're most likely not meant to be in that space any longer. The season has changed and you are being led to your next calling. Don't just stew in that. Move! (DISCLAIMER: Don't walk into that job tomorrow and tell them people that you quit because you're out of alignment. You need to make a plan, but at least you have this as an indication that the time may be up for this assignment).

ASSIGNMENT: noun \ ə-ˈsīn-mənt \

a specified task or amount of work assigned or undertaken as if assigned by an authority

Your alignment is guided by assignments. Consider times where you KNOW you were only somewhere because God had you on an assignment. Where were you? When was the assignment over? How did you know?

_____

_____

_____

_____

_____

_____

_____

13 Can't Keep Running In and Out of My Life

Speaking of alignment and assignments chile, whew. I have had more than my fair share of times where I was way out of alignment with God and my purpose. Let's throw it back to 2007 (trigger warning: violence).

I was a sophomore at Howard, living in my own apartment on Capitol Hill. Kanye West had just dropped the song "Flashing Lights" and I was the girl with the "wood floors in the new apartment / couture from the store's departments." You couldn't tell me nothing. I had met this guy named Bryson who was the perfect combination of thug and comedian (don't ask). He got along well with my closest friends and he was just overall a dope boy - literally.

Bryson was a grocery store manager by day and drug dealer by life. He spent all of his free time selling crack, smoking weed, and listening to UGK (he wanted to be from Texas so bad). He had all of the signs of an abuser but I was too cocky to see it for myself.

There aren't even enough pages available in this book to tell you all of the tea, but let me put it like this: we were together for 4 years. I was happy for 4 months. Don't get it twisted - we had some fun times, but as high as the highs were, the lows were even lower. We had a roller-coaster of a relationship that literally rocked my world and destroyed my confidence.

I experienced a bunch of things while dating Bryson:

- I learned how to cook crack.

- I stayed in a trap house for a few days.

- I learned how to roll a blunt.

- I learned the different types of drugs and how to weigh them.

- I counted over one million dollars by hand.

- I learned how to load and clean a gun.

I knew that Bryson wasn't really my type of dude, but I stayed in the relationship because I was concerned about what would happen if I left. I had seen too much. I remember one day he picked me up from work in his new tricked-out Ford F-150 to take me to lunch. It was a welcomed break from my job at the UNCF. He told me we were going to have lunch at my favorite restaurant in Georgetown. Driving down K Street NW and bumping "She Luv It" by UGK, Bryson was on top of the world. If you aren't familiar with the DC area, K Street is where all of the major lobbyist and advocacy firms have their headquarters. As Pimp C sang, "Slide down slow she getting down on the floor," Bryson abruptly slammed on the brakes and pulled into the driveway of the Capital Hilton. Before I knew it, he had hopped out of the truck and was walking back up K Street yelling at some white man.

Now - let me paint the picture. Bryson was like the size of Rick Ross. Not the new Rick Ross. The OLDDDDDD Rick Ross - like Port of Miami Rick Ross. Standing over 6'2" and caramel complected, he was not someone you could ignore on a street full of slim white men in skinny suits. So to see a bronze Rick Ross walking down K Street in an extra long white tee and sagging jeans - he was just out of place.

Anyway, he starts yelling down the street at a young, white guy in a grey suit. "You just gon' ignore me tho?!" Grey Suit responds, "Aye, B! I've been meaning to call y–." Before Grey Suit could get "you" out of his mouth, there was a loud pop and some screams. Bryson calmly walked back to the truck, got in, cranked up his favorite Houston rappers, and drove off. Yep. I saw Bryson shoot a white man in the leg in the middle of broad daylight on K Street.

As if that wasn't enough crazy to make me leave, fast forward to 2009. We had been together for a minute and I knew wayyyyy too much to get out. It was Super Bowl Sunday and I was doing everything to make Bryson comfortable at home to watch the game. I was in the middle of frying chicken wings when I heard his phone going off. I had sent him down to the basement to grab our clothes out of the dryer. Curiosity got the better of me and I went to see who was sending him so many text messages back-to-back. All I saw was some girl named Tia texting, "Hey babe. Pick up the phone," when the door swung open and Bryson entered huffing and puffing from lugging the laundry basket up the 3 flights of stairs. He dropped the basket on the floor, slammed the door, and before I knew it, I too was on the floor. Honestly, I don't even know how I got there, but I remember using my arms to shield my face as Bryson's kicks landed all over my body. I literally had an out-of-body experience. I was partially shook at the fact that this man had the audacity to put his hands on me. I was also trying to figure out how I, Kendra THEE Y. Hill, was in this situation. Laying in a ball on my living room floor and squinting through my tears, I watched Bryson walk toward the kitchen.

As my adrenaline pumped ferociously through my body, I got off of the floor and ran towards an unassuming Bryson. Chile, I was up and I was stuck. There was no way this man was getting away with this. I jumped on his back and started hitting him in the head and clawing at his eyes. With the force of ten elephants, he threw me off of his back but I landed on my feet with the precision of a cat. I ran into the bedroom and slammed and locked the door while Bryson tried to regain his senses. In a fit of rage, I considered the only way I could get back at him that would really piss him off. Running to the closet, I grabbed a handful of his designer goods and rushed to the window. Before I knew it, the alley was littered with his things. Watching the snow fall on his precious Gucci sunglasses and red bottom sneakers brought me so much joy. Long story short, Bryson went to retrieve his things before the crackheads got to them and I locked my front door and cleaned up the burnt fried chicken and Crisco in the kitchen.

Now I know you're probably thinking, "Kendra, this story is too wild. I KNOW you left after this." NOPE. I didn't. And the worst part of all of this was that I felt like I deserved this. It's sad, I know.

The final straw came while I was away on a business trip. I was working at a UNCF Board Meeting at Tuskegee University when Bryson slept with two different girls at my house in my bed. He also got both girls pregnant. #FullSTOP

I didn't know how I was going to get out of the situation, but I knew that I couldn't take any more of the abuse. I ended up interviewing for a job with Google back in Texas and getting the position. I never told Bryson; I convinced him that I was going to visit my mom for the summer and I'd be back. Needless to say, I packed two suitcases and never returned. Bryson stayed at my place over the summer while I "visited home" until he got the eviction notice. I was so far out of alignment that I was ready to risk it all, including my credit, to get out of the situation.

There are so many signs when you're out of place. Sometimes it's being at the wrong job and other times it's being in the wrong situationship, but trust that God is going to make sure that you know that you're trippin'. It's not God's plan that you are out of place. Let's talk about indicators.

INDICATORS: noun \ ˈin-də- ̱kā-tər \

a thing, especially a trend or fact, that indicates the state or level of something

God uses nudges and signs as indicators that you're either moving in the right direction or that you're off course. If we look back at my time at the Spurs, God used my consistent discontent as a sign or indication of the fact that it was time to move on. When I reflect on my relationship with Bryson, being in the trap house was the first real indicator that I ignored (silly me).

Now, let me say this before we get into these indicators: it's normal for us to fall in and out of alignment with God. I'm not saying it's okay, but it IS normal. Even some of the greatest prophets in the bible fell out of alignment at times. Consider Elijah running from Jezebel (he was just scared), or Jonah running from Nineveh (he didn't think the Ninevites deserved mercy), or Moses striking the rock instead of speaking to it (he was TIDE - not tired, but TIDE). Different things pop up in our lives that cause us to get unaligned.

Some indicators that you are aligned are:

- Things feel calm around you.

- Money flows in easily.

- Things you have been trying to manifest seem to fall on your lap.

- Ultimately, you have peace.

Some indicators that you aren't aligned are:

- Feelings of heightened anxiety and worry.

- Pushing hard to get things done with no real results.

- A lack of motivation/ambition.

- Things seemingly keep "going wrong".

- You generally feel disconnected from yourself.

- You wake up often feeling like something is "off".

Sometimes it's hard to even recognize that we're out of place. I typically attribute this to a lack of intimacy with God. Because life IS tough and we DO go through trials, it's easy to struggle with surrendering to God. A lot of people just stop obeying altogether. Do you want me to expose your own barriers to intimacy with God and dismantle them? Yes? NO?! Doesn't matter - let's get into it.

- LACK OF TRUST - This is the number one thing that keeps us from being close to God and ultimately gets us out of alignment. We get so caught up in what hasn't happened or hasn't manifested that we start to feel like God is a liar. Numbers 23:19 cleared that up for us ("God is not a man that He should lie. Neither the son of man that He should repent..."). The easiest way to clear this up is to spend more time with Him so that you can trust His character again.

- BLAME - Yikes! We've all been there. Something bad happens and now we want to make God be the villain in our telenovela. We blame God for our suffering or the pain we've endured when in reality, we probably need to accept some accountability for what we've done. It's important for us to be able to accept that things happen in life that are indeed beyond our control, but God takes everything and turns it around for our good. Even your lowest points in life are for your good (Romans 8:28).

- GUILT AND SHAME - This is a big one, especially when we feel like we've really messed up. But let me help you:

  - GUILT is when you feel bad for what you've done. But there's literally no reason to walk around feeling guilty. 1 John 1:9 KJV says, "If we confess our sins, he is faithful and just to forgive us our sins, and to cleanse us from all unrighteousness." Soooooo what you running for?

  - SHAME is when you feel bad about who you are or what has happened to you. The enemy is good at making those who have suffered sexual abuse feel like they should be ashamed. Issa no for me, dawg. Romans 8:1 is clear that "there is no condemnation in Christ Jesus" so you have no reason to be out here feeling like a leper. PERIODT.

- LACK OF SHARING - A lot of people suffer from pride when it comes to prayer and communicating with God. It's like we don't want to tell God the truth about how we feel, but I've learned that being honest and transparent with Him is the best route. At the end of the day, He already knows! So when you pray, share your highs, lows, and in-betweens - even if it's about your relationship with Him. John 4:24 reminds us that we must worship Him (intimacy) in spirit AND in TRUTH.

- LACK OF OBEDIENCE - This is spicy but it's 10000000% true. Folks be out here dipping out on God because they won't obey and I don't like that. I don't like it for God, but I also don't like it for you. God is constantly talking and giving instructions. It's up to us to obey what He's saying even when we don't like it. Delayed obedience is still disobedience and prolonged disobedience is rebellion and rebellion is likened to witchcraft. Okay, bye! (Study Ephesians 5:6 and 1 Samuel 15:23 when you're ready to deal with this).

- SELFISHNESS - We don't like to admit it, but most of us are very selfish when we go before God in prayer. We can't make moments of intimacy with God about us alone. It's like intimacy in marriage - every encounter can't just be for your pleasure! In the words of the psalmist Mystikal, "Do yo' thang don't be scared, cause you gon' get served. You get mine then you gon' get yours!" God will grant you the desires of your heart, but you have to approach Him as the sovereign and understand that you're His child - not His equal! (Oh - Romans 8:5 might help with this).

Back to these indicators: It's our job to be attentive to the signs in the world around us. Are you listening? If you've gone 12 months and life hasn't changed, you're probably going the wrong way. We all go through tough seasons but it's our perseverance through those seasons that strengthen us. So if you've gone a whole year cycle without change, reconsider your path. You might need to take some time to consult your creator and head back to the drawing board! Remember, alignment in your assignment is the MEANS to fulfilling your PURPOSE!

Take some time to reflect on your life. Where are you right now? What feelings do you get when you think about work? How do you feel about the place you live in? How do you feel about the work you do? The people you keep around you? Where's your intimacy with God? Again, there are different seasons for things in our lives. Do a temperature check with yourself. You might find out you aren't aligned with where you're supposed to be. What can you do to pivot?

_____

_____

_____

_____

_____

_____

_____

_____

_____

_____

_____

_____

_____

_____

_____

_____

_____

I Can Read Your Mind

Honestly, I could have started this whole book talking about mindset. I was having a conversation with one of my clients the other day about changing the thought patterns in your mind and I realized that my mindset didn't change when I became a millionaire; my mindset changed when I stepped into therapy for the first time. (Disclaimer: I am not licensed to give psychological advice. The following opinion is based on my decade-long journey in therapy. I also was the COO of the largest mental health clinic in Canada, sooooo…).

I was a freshman at Howard when I knew I needed some help. My mental health had probably been rapidly declining since I was 8 years old, but it wasn't until I was raped by my watchcare pastor at 19 that I was willing to take the steps necessary to get my mind on track. I wasn't blaming myself for the assault, but it triggered the memories of my grandfather/father raping me and that pain was unbearable.

Tamika was not your typical therapist. She didn't play about God and she didn't play about homework. She was perfect for me. We probably spent the first 10 sessions diving into my history. While it was easy to tell her all of the hard stories, it was hard to hear that it wasn't my fault. I guess I had spent the rest of my childhood convincing myself that I must have done something wrong to have deserved the pain I suffered. Undoing my negative thoughts about my past was only the beginning.

As I journeyed with Tamika, I processed a lot about myself. I learned that I was deeply analytical, somewhat cynical, and extremely critical of everything and everyone around me. I had no grace for myself or others and I couldn't find compassion if Jesus Himself came down and handed it to me. I was a wreck. Week after week I would go to her office on H Street NE in DC and turn into a puddle on her couch.

One day, Tamika said, "You know you're really supposed to be someone great, right?" I sat still looking out the window at the construction happening across the street. I couldn't accept that I had a purpose. Even though my godmother had spent so much time pumping me up, life had worked overtime to knock me down. My mind was running a marathon, but the room was so quiet, you could hear a rat piss on cotton in a Catholic church. I couldn't produce a single sound. After an uncomfortable amount of silence, Tamika interrupted my negative self-talk with, "God has called you for something great. You're gonna have money. Like MONEY money." That was when I compartmentalized the "prophetic" talks with Tamika and labeled them as senseless rants. "You came from nothing and you're gonna be nothing," I thought to myself.

Fast forward all of these years later and I've apologized to Tamika. She's still my therapist and she's still speaking into my life. After 2-3 years of therapy, she started helping me shift my mind to professional development and goal-setting. My time with her in my mid-20s was focused on shifting my mind to receive abundance and wealth in every aspect of my life.

Mindset shifts start with you. This journey to purpose takes a lot of mental strength and stamina. You have to tap into mindfulness.

MINDFULNESS: noun \ ˈmīn(d)-fəl-nəs \

the practice of maintaining a nonjudgmental state of heightened or complete awareness of one's thoughts, emotions, or experiences on a moment-to-moment basis

This is why "there's so much room for activities" in this book (Stepbrothers is one of my favorite movies lol). Each one of us is in a different place when it comes to our mindset around our purpose. Versus experiencing a rigid journey, you've spent the last 13 chapters roaming and meandering and playing so you can fully experience mindfulness. It's time to go a bit deeper. Follow the prompts (in order - no cheating!) and see where your imagination takes you.

At this point, I want you to consider your purpose. How you felt at the beginning of this book and what you may know now should be a little different. So hone in on your purpose and answer the following:

What is it that you feel you were made to be doing?

_____

_____

_____

_____

_____

_____

_____

What is one thing that everyone counts on you for? Is it the same as your Golden Spoon? Do they work together?

_____

_____

_____

_____

_____

_____

_____

_____

_____

What do you seem to be thinking about most of your time during the day and what is that one thing you always talk about?

_____

_____

_____

_____

_____

_____

_____

Now, think about your goals. Regardless of when you're reading this book, you probably have a list of goals that you want to accomplish in the near future. What do you imagine feeling at the end of this year?

_____

_____

_____

_____

_____

_____

_____

What do you want to be doing in your business next year?

_____

_____

_____

_____

_____

_____

_____

_____

Let's shift into faith and gratitude. How often do you communicate and express gratitude to God? (Be HONEST).

_____

_____

_____

_____

_____

_____

_____

What is He saying to you right now?

_____

_____

_____

_____

_____

_____

_____

How do you keep gratitude in front of you?

_____

_____

_____

_____

_____

_____

_____

Now for a real challenge. Let's talk about limiting beliefs. I remember when I used to think that I couldn't be an influencer because I was fat (ha-haha). What do you think is one thing that is stopping you from achieving your goals?

_____

_____

_____

_____

_____

_____

_____

What are your weaknesses?

_____

_____

_____

_____

_____

_____

_____

_____

How do you think your weaknesses can be improved or translated to serve for good?

_____

_____

_____

_____

_____

_____

_____

Motivation: Why do you want to walk in purpose?

_____

_____

_____

_____

_____

_____

_____

How do you imagine feeling once you start fully walking in your purpose?

_____

_____

_____

_____

_____

_____

_____

What do you want your life to be like in 10 years? 20 years? Why?

_____

_____

_____

_____

_____

_____

Determination: Is your current path going to aid in who you want to become?

_____

_____

_____

_____

_____

_____

_____

_____

What decisions are you making right now that will help you walk in purpose for the rest of your life?

_____

_____

_____

_____

_____

_____

_____

_____

How good are you at letting go and leaning into things you can't ignore? Are you ready to do that?

_____

_____

_____

_____

_____

_____

_____

_____

We know that purpose is impact, so let's talk about service to others. What is something that you are doing to help or inspire others right now?

_____

_____

_____

_____

_____

_____

_____

What would you want to be doing for others in the future?

_____

_____

_____

_____

_____

_____

_____

When you think about how you are most helpful, what activity are you doing? Is it assisting someone with their project? Is it being a shoulder to cry on? Who are you when you're being helpful?

_____

_____

_____

_____

_____

_____

_____

There are two major factors that contribute to your ability to get to the next level: risk and consistency. When was the last time you took a big risk and what results did you get?

_____

_____

_____

_____

_____

_____

When it comes to taking calculated risks, what is your decision-making process?

_____

_____

_____

_____

_____

_____

128 How well do you recover after failing in something that was risky?

PURPOSE-DRIVEN ENTERPRISE

_____

_____

_____

_____

_____

_____

_____

What is the one thing in your life (personal or professional) that you are consistent about?

_____

_____

_____

_____

_____

_____

What results did you get from being consistent?

_____

_____

_____

_____

_____

_____

_____

_____

Where else would you like to apply that consistency in your life?

_____

_____

_____

_____

_____

_____

15 It's Kanye's Workout Plan

I know you didn't expect to get advice on weight loss from a fat girl, but here it is. I realized years ago that at times, my purpose would require me to do something physically challenging. Back then, it was casting out demons during a deliverance service. Now, it's traveling on an intense schedule (there are literal months where I'm on the road for 15-20 days).

It was 2014 when it become clear that I had to get myself in better shape. I had just moved to Sacramento, California from DC as God was trying to excommunicate me from my hood life as a crack-slanging madame. After three months of living in Sac, I had acclimated to a new lifestyle on the west coast. I was walking everywhere and eating organic anything. Jamba Juice was my best friend and I knew the owner of just about every farm-to-table restaurant. Over the course of 9 months, I lost 90 pounds and went from a size 20 to a 12.

About halfway through those 9 months, I had one of the scariest experiences of my life. I was on my way to the grocery store when I blacked out. Yep. I passed out right at the intersection of Mack Road and Franklin Boulevard. When I opened my eyes, an El Pollo Loco employee was tapping me and loudly yelling, "Ma'am? Ma'am, are you alright." I laid there for a minute in shock. Did I really pass out in the street? Still lying on the ground, I grabbed the back of my head to check for blood. "Nothing there, thank God," I thought to myself as I checked the rest of my body for scrapes and bruises. I sat up slowly and thanked the young man who brought me back to consciousness. He ran back to his job and brought me a big cup of water (honestly, thank GOD for this dude. There's a Popeye's there now, so we KNOW that wouldn't happen today lol). I got up off of the ground, called my mom, and took my tail back home.

A few days passed and I was feeling fine. I had been pretty gentle with myself after the blackout. I didn't want to have another episode and possibly hurt myself even more. And then it happened again. I was getting out of bed and the next thing I know, my dog Snow was licking my hand to wake me up. At least this time I was at home on the carpet, but waking up on the floor again was just unacceptable. This time, my angel was a white Maltipoo who knew not to lick me but used her doggy wisdom to help me. I knew it was time to get help.

A visit to the doctor made it clear that I was losing weight too fast. I was actually more unhealthy at a size 16 than I was when I was over 300 pounds. Dr. Hoover recommended that I slowly add more carbohydrates back into my diet and stopped consuming caffeine altogether. For the first time in my life, I understood that weight was not the prime indicator of health.

Health really is wealth, y'all. You can't complete the assignments that God has given you if you aren't doing the basic things to take care of yourself. This means drinking lots of water (I do 2 liters a day), sleeping for 8+ hours a night (Lord, I need you to help me lol), and getting at least 30 minutes of exercise in each day (I manage lol). And don't get me started on diet. Folks think I hired my chef because I'm flexing. NO. I hired her because I needed someone to help me stay on track with eating three clean meals a day. I'm also doing better at taking my vitamins and supplements. As my mom says, "I'd rather take 100 vitamins a day than 1 drug." So it's time to examine your overall health. Let's get into it!

When's the last time you had a physical? Be honest?

_____

_____

What about your gynocologist (if you're a woman) or urologist (if you're a man)? When's the last time you saw them?

_____

_____

If it's over a year for either of these questions, I need you to go and get these check-ups scheduled ASAP. Do you have any pre-existing health conditions that you need to be monitoring? What are they and what should you be doing?

_____

_____

_____

_____

_____

_____

_____

_____

Do you have a specific diet that you would like to be following? Outline it below.

_____

_____

_____

_____

_____

_____

_____

Right here, I want you to commit to drinking at least 2 liters of water a day. Yep. We're creating a contracted standard right here in the middle of this book.

I _____ *(full name)* am committed to drinking AT LEAST 2 liters of water per day. On days that I miss the mark, I will give myself grace, but I am making a promise to myself (and Kendra Y. Hill) that I will do my absolute best.

_____

Signature

_____

Date

Close Every Door to Me

Back in Chapter 10, I told y'all that it was so important to keep God-centered people around you. In those times when you can't see what's next or you're feeling low, a good circle will keep you going. As my client Lucinda Cross says, "There's power in the circle."

But what if I told you that cutting people off in droves may be a part of your purpose process? Picture it: Dallas. August 2018 lol. I was in a real transitional place in my life and I was questioning God for the next move. I felt like I was supposed to move to Nashville, Tennessee, but I was uncertain. Nashville is what you think it is - country. And country just ain't my steeze. I have nothing against the country music capital of the world, but Nashville really just wasn't my vibe (and still ain't).

In addition to Makiyah and Nixon, I had a prayer team that we affectionately called "The 6" - partially because there were six of them, but also because I love Drake and "I was running through The 6 with my woes!" The 6 prayed for me daily during this season of my life. I felt lost, but I knew that God was telling me to make a move. At the end of each day, they would text or email me if they got a word from the Lord. Most of the major shifts and directions were given to me directly from God through my dreams, but their details added some color to the Lord's outline.

"Who is this that is experiencing kidney failure? They gotta go," Diahana said casually. It was so intense we had to have a conference call and one by one, they started rattling off signs and descriptions to help me compile the list of people I had to distance myself from. Pam remarked, "There's a woman who poured into you as a child. God said that she's speaking word curses over your marriage." Another one bites the dust. Enoch brought up someone I had forgotten about. "You have a childhood friend who was a kleptomaniac. She's outta here too." Welp, bye-bye Connie! Every person mentioned was a door that I had to close. Beyond the accuracy of their advice, I was shook at the confirmation that it gave me.

No one knew, but I had a dream a week or so before about this. In this dream, Nixon and I were visiting a famous gospel music couple at their studio in Los Angeles. Though we knew these people in real life, this visit seemed weird. All four of us had on white and we stood outside of the studio speaking affirmations over each other. Nixon and I got in our car and drove to a chateausesque two-story home in Beverly Hills. We entered the house and went upstairs to the master suite when I heard the voice of the Lord. "You must close every door before 9." Then I looked out the window and saw a raging flood outside with our home as its target. I took off running around the second story of our home shutting every literal door before racing downstairs to close those doors too. I could hear the floodwaters getting closer to my house and I couldn't bear the thought of everything we had built being swept away. I secured the front door of the house just as the water reached our property. I raced back upstairs and closed the french doors to our suite just as the water slammed into our home and the clock struck 9:00 pm.

When I woke up, I knew that I had some strenuous mission ahead of me, but again, The 6 gave me all of the details that I needed. Getting off of that conference call was tough. I actually didn't know what "9" was. Was it actually nine o'clock or was it September, the 9th month of the year? I wasn't sure what it was, but by the time I finished playing Guess Who, I had a list of 32+ people who had to be removed from me. Some of them were just for a season and I'm reconnected to them right now. Some of them were for a lifetime.

You can only imagine how those calls went. "Hey, Danny! Love you but the Lord said I gotta cut you off." Danny took it well. He was a man of God and He understood that seasons changed. An old crush, Micah, was outraged. "WTF do you mean you can't speak to me? I told you I respect your man. Why you buggin'?" Other people I just blocked on social media and in my phone. Some people wanted to have conversations with me about it. Regardless, I knew that I had to close these open doors.

OPEN DOOR: noun \ 'ō-pən'dȯr \

an access point to the enemy via sin or ungodly soul ties

You might be reading this and feeling confused, but let me help you. Imagine you left the front door wide open to your house for a week. Not only would you probably get some critters sneaking in, but you could also have someone come into your home and do some damage. You'd be leaving everything open and available to any intruder. Your valuables. Your belongings. Everything.

Well, we do this same thing spiritually. We leave open doors for the enemy all the time. You're probably familiar with the scripture in 1 Peter 5:8 KJV: "Be sober, be vigilant; because your adversary the devil, as a roaring lion, walketh about, seeking whom he may devour." So the devil is always looking for ways to get you off track and ultimately destroy you. The problem is that most of us willingly give him access to our valuables by leaving our doors wide open.

Most times, we willingly invite the devil into our lives via sin. When we are outside of the will of God, we allow the enemy to invade our lives. It's an open invitation. But sometimes, those open doors come through attachments and ungodly soul ties.

SOUL TIE: noun \ 'sōl 'tī \

a spiritual or emotional connection you have to someone after being intimate with them; usually (but not always) through sexual activity.

The Bible makes it plain in 1 Corinthians 6:16 AMP: "Do you not know that the one who joins himself to a prostitute is one body with her?"

Do you have them? Bodies? Most of us think that we don't. Most of us think that we have moved on from Brandon or Kenneth or Vanessa or

Karen, but we haven't. We feel like we've gotten over our ex-boyfriends/ girlfriends, ex-husbands/wives, old flings, cut buddies, etc. when we delete their phone numbers and stop texting them. I'm here to tell you that we're sadly mistaken. There are deeper, spiritual attachments that we're holding on to. But again, soul ties aren't JUST sexual and romantic situations. Here are three types of soul ties that we usually encounter:

1. **Sexual Relations:** The bible says in Ephesians 5:31 AMP: "For this reason a man shall leave his father and mother and be joined to his wife, and the two shall become one flesh." This is an example of a Godly soul tie. When GOD joins two people together, no man can break that tie. Marriage is not marriage unless or until there is consummation; yes, hanky panky. Marriage is a covenant. There is no covenant unless there is bloodshed (according to Genesis 15:9-21), which is why you're supposed to save your body for marriage - but that's a WHOLE different conversation. Ungodly sexual relations (outside of marriage) create a soul tie. They are destructive and break down your soul. If you've had many sexual partners, it can be difficult to be able to attach to anyone; even the person you were MADE for.

2. **Close Relationships:** One of the greatest examples of a Godly, positive soul tie can be found in King David and Jonathan. 1 Samuel 18:1 AMP says, "When David had finished speaking to Saul, the soul of Jonathan was bonded to the soul of David, and Jonathan loved him as himself." Though this is a Godly soul tie, bad soul ties can be formed from relationships as well. When you begin to idolize someone or desire to be like them (our generation calls it "#goals"), a bad tie can be formed. Even something like idolizing a celebrity can create an ungodly soul tie that needs to be broken.

3. **Vows, Commitments, and Agreements:** Vows at a wedding bind souls together, but what about business agreements? Numbers 30:2 AMP declares, "If a man makes a vow to the Lord or swears an oath to bind himself with a pledge, he shall

not break (violate, profane) his word; he shall do according to all that proceeds out of his mouth." If this is true (which we know God's word is), then business agreements, promises, pacts, etc. are all subject to being a soul tie.

So I want you to take inventory of your own life. Make a list of every person you've shared intimacy with. Could be sexual. Could be emotional. We know the importance of writing things down, so actually MAKE the list. Do an inventory of your body count. To be honest, when I made my own list, there were names I couldn't remember (don't judge me and I won't judge you), so I put the situation on the list.

TAKE YOUR TIME. This exercise could take you a few days and that's okay. Every time I've done this (yes, I make it a part of my annual cleaning), I've actually felt physically sick. Probably because I realized that most of these soul ties were my own fault.

_____   _____

_____   _____

_____   _____

_____   _____

_____   _____

_____   _____

_____   _____

_____   _____

_____   _____

_____   _____

_____   _____

_____   _____

Now, take a moment to pray and ask God if there are any current attachments that need to be removed. Jot down whatever you hear.

_____

_____

_____

_____

_____

_____

_____

17 Think I Better Let It Go. Looks Like Another Love T.K.O.

By now you know that I'm thorough, so we aren't exactly done with open doors and soul ties. We're going to destroy them now because there's no point in holding on. Before I get into my story, let me explain why we're even talking about this so deeply. I learned years ago that I cannot fully walk in my purpose or reach my fullest potential if I'm still connected to people and things that are not meant for me. God will not bless you with everything you're supposed to have if you're still attached to people who don't deserve to reap the benefits of those blessings. I couldn't become a multimillionaire until I destroyed every ungodly attachment. The people I was connected with would have proverbially raped and pillaged me the moment I had an extra comma in my bank account. I couldn't fully walk in purpose connected to people who were selling drugs, worshipping other gods, and honoring their flesh more than their spirit. It wasn't possible.

Anyway, let me tell you about Omar. We met when I was working on Capitol Hill and just hit it off immediately. I was dating Bryson at the time (the fake Freeway Ricky Ross) so Omar and I were really just friends. He was working on The Hill full-time and working on music projects at night. Over the course of 5 years, our friendship grew from just colleagues to friends and ultimately lovers. Bryson was cheating on me with a bunch of girls and I was cheating on him with Omar (I was wild back in my day lol). Once Bryson slept with those two girls while I was on a business trip, I started having some "business trips" of my own. I would tell Bryson that I had to travel for work and then I'd show up at the Marriott Wardman Park for a sexscapade with Omar.

Over time we fell in love, and once I had escaped to Texas to work at Google, we were officially an item. I'll spare you the details, but because I was still broken from my relationship with my father (not knowing the truth but still feeling so rejected), I was ecstatic when Omar proposed to me over Skype. Yep. I accepted a Skype proposal.

That moment led to me moving back to DC for a bit. Omar and I were growing at a steady pace but secretly, he was battling drug addiction. His best friend ended up telling me about it (because he also liked me and wanted me to leave Omar to be with him smh). I stayed with Omar while he went to inpatient rehab where he wrote me letters like he was in prison. Hindsight being 20/20, I can't even wrap my mind around this situation.

Anyway, once he got out of rehab, we tried to rebuild our relationship, but all we really had in common was sex. We were breaking records for intimacy and orgasms and with everything I was managing in my own business, that was enough for me. Ultimately, our relationship ended shortly after LaToya (remember her?) moved in with me and started stirring the pot. I later found out that she wanted to be with Omar - I mean, they WERE both drug addicts, so it may have worked out.

One summer day in 2013, Omar called and told me that it was over; that he didn't want to be with me anymore and we weren't getting married. He told me I could keep everything he gave me including my ring, but it was over. I didn't cry. I didn't beg. I just accepted it. Honestly, I knew that we were just never going to work long term but I didn't want to break up with my friend. We went years without talking - partially because of the breakup and partially because I started to see how much the drugs had impacted his cognitive skills. I just couldn't take seeing him like that even though he had dumped me.

Obviously, I moved on and literally moved to California where I finally got myself aligned with God frfr, but Omar never really moved on. It took him a few years to reach out, but in 2021, I got a random text that read, "Aye u." After inquiring a bit, I figured out that it was him, but I didn't know what he wanted. He played it off like a friendly check-in, but I knew there was something more that he wanted. Sure enough, a few weeks went by and he started calling my phone. I ignored him for a while because I just didn't want to deal with THAT open door. I didn't have any feelings for him. I was with Nixon and could care less about what Omar had going on.

He was pretty persistent with his contact so I finally arranged a day and time to chat. The conversation started off fine, but it went a la izquierda (to the left) real quick. Omar wanted me back. No surprise there, but I wasn't gonna let him in. "I miss you. I miss sex with you. You were so passionate in bed." That was it for me. I kindly dismissed Omar and blocked his number. A week or so later, he started following me on Instagram. I blocked him there, too. And chile, he created a new Instagram account about 3 weeks ago (literally, as I'm writing this) and followed me again. BLOCKEDT.

Omar's constant pressure to connect was a reminder that I needed to really let him go and do a soul tie detox specifically for him. Our closeness, both sexually and emotionally, was a MAJOR open door that I hadn't really dealt with. Omar was really out of sight, out of mind for me, but in the realm of the spirit, that connection was still there.

So let me share 6 steps to getting delivered from these deadly soul ties. Take your time and make sure that you actually fulfill the steps. Don't just breeze through them. You'll find that as you work through this process, you'll feel lighter and even more connected to God.

1. REPENT! A lot of ungodly soul ties are formed via committing sin. If you fornicated with someone, repent. If getting drunk or high was what bound y'all together, repent. If lying, stealing, etc. were a part of the relationship, repent. I know that you're all deep and wonderful and repent daily, but I want you to dig into the list you made in the last chapter and repent of each of those things you may have done with those people.

2. TRASH IT! I know that it's common to keep mementos and items as personal memories. Sometimes because you just love the thing; sometimes to be spiteful (I was like that with my engagement ring from my Omar); sometimes because you just can't let go. Perhaps you bought something with the per-

son, they bought something for you, or you got something together - whatever the case may be, you MUST get rid of it. I've received jewelry, cards, flowers, lingerie, clothes, etc. from people who I had soul ties with. TRASHED! Clothes that my ex-friends bought for me. TRASHED! Don't hang on to any reminders that you have of the people or the acts performed. It's a necessary part of your detox.

Let's pause here. I want you to write down your feelings about this process so far. How do you feel about letting go of these items?

_____

_____

_____

_____

_____

_____

_____

3. GUARD YOUR MOUTH! Sometimes we make rash vows when we're caught up and in love. I myself have told a man before, "I will always love you" or, "I'll love you forever" or, "I could never love anyone as much as I love you". Those are all vows that have to be broken. Telling some man who broke your heart, hurt your feelings, and is no longer in the picture that you "could never love anyone as much as you love him" completely shuts out the true love you're supposed to have (ultimately blocking you from fulfilling your purpose as well). Telling someone that you will love them forever (and them oftentimes reciprocating) can cause your heart to become hard and bitter. Imagine not being able to truly be open and free with the person that God has for you because your heart is

occupied or hardened. Just like we know that life and death are in the power of your tongue, so is the key to breaking these ungodly bonds.

From this step, I'd like for you to do this: write out a prayer asking God to empty your heart of anything that isn't of/from Him. Also, include in your prayer that you want God to turn your heart of stone into a heart of flesh as indicated in Ezekiel 36:26.

This step is important because you may have done/said the above affirmations by mistake without realizing their impact. Make sure that you jot down other notes on your journey (i.e. how you're feeling, any strange things that have happened, etc.).

_____

_____

_____

_____

_____

_____

_____

4. FORGIVE! I know that sounds so simple, but harboring ill feelings or feelings of guilt, shame, hurt, etc. will cause you to be stuck right where you are. Sometimes we hold things against people without even realizing that's what we're doing. There is a crazy amount of freedom in forgiveness. I told you about how strained my relationship was with my mom as a child. I walked around for all of my teenage years and even my early twenties holding resentment against her because I felt she rejected me. There was a negative tie with her that I had to break and it began with forgiving her.

We're always told "forgive and forget" or "forgive or forget" when honestly, that's a major challenge for most of us. I had to ask God to help me to forgive my mother for seemingly neglecting me. To help me to forgive my grandfather/father for molesting me. Forgiveness is challenging, BUT it frees you to move on in your life. The emotions that come with forgiving someone can be difficult, but the feelings of unforgiveness are brutal. This doesn't necessarily mean that you have to (or should) talk to the person and tell them that you are forgiving them, but should you choose to do so, keep it brief and to the point. Don't engage to reconnect.

This next exercise is a challenge. I want you to write out a letter forgiving everyone who has ever wronged you in anyway. It can be as long or as short as you want, but write out how Bobby raped you, or how Jessica manipulated you and then left you, or how your father was never there. THEN, forgive them. In order to get free from your bondage, you have to forgive others; not for them, but for you. You can write whatever you need to write. This letter isn't meant to be delivered, so be as honest and frank as you need to.

_____

_____

_____

_____

_____

_____

_____

_____

_____

_____

THINK I BETTER LET IT GO. LOOKS LIKE ANOTHER LOVE T.K.O.

Whew! We're almost there. The bible says in Romans 10:17 KJV that "faith cometh by hearing, and hearing by the word of God." So now it's time to speak out loud so that your faith can be activated by hearing.

5. RENOUNCE! This simply means to formally declare your abandonment of something. Be sure to do this for EACH person on your list. We're going to do this right now by way of making a verbal declaration in Jesus' name:

"In Jesus' name, I now renounce any ungodly soul ties formed between myself and _____ as a result of _____ (fornication, etc.)."

If the sin is the same for multiple people, you can say it once (i.e. between myself and Bryson, Omar, Kevin, and David as a result of fornication).

6. PRAY! Now it's time to break the soul tie! Pray this prayer for yourself:

"I renounce all covenants, pacts, promises, curses and every other work of darkness to which I have been exposed or made liable by my own actions or by the actions of others. By the act and decision of my own free will, Father, in the name of Jesus, I ask You to go to the root and dig, cut, tear and loose me from every soul-tie and from every form of bondage of my soul and body to satan, or any of his agents rather in human form or demonic form or animal form. And Father, in the name of Jesus, I also, ask that You go to each of the above named, and at the root, dig, tear, cut and loose them from me. Take and detach me from them, and detach them from and out of me, in Jesus' name!

Father God, in the name of Jesus Christ, thank you for the authority of Your Word. In the name of Jesus: I command every portion of my soul (my thoughts, my will, my emotions, my personality, and mind) and heart, all of me: spirit, soul, and body, that has been fragmented, torn or broken or cursed, to come back into its proper place. To be healed. That every piece of my heart be returned, my soul to be restored, and every bondage and related soul-tie to be completely broken, destroyed and totally detached from me, in the name of Jesus!

Father God, in the name of Jesus, I ask now, that You heal my heart and guard it by Your Power and Your Love, and keep my heart and mind through Christ Jesus. Make me every which way whole in every area of my life. I desire to live in a manner that pleases You, and brings glory to Your name. I choose now to present my body to the Lord, as a living sacrifice, as the scriptures recommend, and to walk in holiness as You, Lord Jesus, enable me to do so.

I come before the throne of grace, Lord Jesus, and confess that I have sinned by doing _____. I now recognize that these were wrong, and I am truly sorry for them. I repent and ask Your forgiveness. I also ask forgiveness for those whom I have wronged or abused. I forgive all those who have wronged or abused me, from birth, and from this day forward, I release them and myself to Your mercy and grace. Please forgive me for all I did and wash all sin and guilt and shame and damage from me with Your blood. I accept and receive Your merciful forgiveness, and purpose in my heart that I will do all in my power to walk in righteousness, with Your help. In Jesus' name, Amen."

That's it! You're free!!

Now, it would be irresponsible of me to give you all of that information and not teach you how to maintain your deliverance from these soul ties. This is where I'm at now - maintenance. Omar was the last ungodly soul tie that I needed to deal with, so not it's up to me to maintain my freedom.

PURPOSE-DRIVEN ENTERPRISE

- DON'T. LOOK. BACK! It may feel really good right now to be free, but the key to deliverance is consistency. No matter WHAT happens, don't go back to those tainted, ungodly relationships. When they call, ignore it. When they text, delete it. In fact, BLOCK THEM!

- REPEAT! If you start feeling "some type of way" again, repeat the detox. You have all of the steps and know what to do. Just detox again if you start feeling contaminated.

- READ AND READ SOME MO! Go back through your journal and remember the feelings of freedom you once experienced. That alone should send you right back down the road to cut the ties.

- KILL THE NEW ONES! New ties will form over time...that's natural. When they do, KILL THEM immediately! Don't allow yourself to fall deep into the trap with new people.

Shut Up! Already. Dang!

Now that we've separated from the hard things, it's time to get into silencing some of the other things in your life.

On Sunday, January 9, 2022, my Instagram and Facebook accounts were hacked. I was cooking dinner in my kitchen when I got a notification that someone had tried to log in to my Facebook account in Thailand. I immediately walked over to my computer and checked my page to see what was happening. Everything looked normal, so I grabbed my phone, denied access to the Thai intruder, and went back to preparing my cajun salmon. Less than five minutes later, I got another message from Facebook saying that someone in Singapore was trying to access my account. This time when I went over to my Macbook to verify everything, my page was gone. Scrambling, I logged into @iamkendrayhill on Instagram and it was gone, too. I got a message saying that my account had been suspended because it violated community guidelines. WHAT!?!

A few minutes later, one of my close friends sent me a text message informing me that someone had sent her child pornography from my account. There it was - the reason I was shut down. Frustrated, I asked my mom (who was visiting at the time) to finish cooking the meal while I tried to recover my account. After thirty minutes of poking and prodding, it was clear that I wasn't getting my account back that night. I sent a text to my friend Lindsey who had just recovered her accounts after nearly a month of being without social media. "You have to join this Meta group on Facebook -" I cut her off before she finished to let her know that my Facebook was gone. That was that.

I knew that I had a direct contact over at Meta who had helped me with some stuff for one of my clients, so I shot an email over to Tómas:

> Hey hey, Tómas!
>
> I'm Kendra - [redacted's] manager. I hope you're doing well.
>
> I know you helped us with a FB account a few weeks ago. I was hoping you could help me. I have 2-factor auth and alerts set up and somehow, someone has hacked my FB account which has also shut down my IG account. You can only imagine how frustrating this is for me.
>
> I went through the recovery steps but I keep hitting a dead end. Please let me know if you could help me or give me some direction.
>
> Thanks!
>
> Kendra

I got an auto-reply message that said Tómas was away on vacation until the end of the week. Honestly, I wasn't sure how long I could go without having my Instagram account. I was scheduled to re-open the enrollment to The Milli Club that week and not having my main account was throwing a major wrench in my plans. I quickly decided to create a new account with the handle @theekendrayhill. I knew that my account being gone was a temporary hurdle that I needed to overcome. I went right into recovery mode by drafting an email to my mailing list, making posts on my new page about my lost page, and praying. God must have had a reason and a plan for all of this.

The purpose of my digital inconvenience was quickly revealed. God wanted me to be still and silent while He gave me instructions. I knew that I was supposed to work on *Purpose-Driven Enterprise* but I had already made some excuses in my mind as to why I wasn't going to put it out until the end of the year: People would buy it around Black Friday. I needed more time to process my own experience. I just didn't want to do it.

Though these excuses were swirling around in my mind like vanilla and chocolate soft serve, I knew that I didn't really have much of a choice.

When you fully surrender and submit to God's will and His purpose in your life, you ultimately exchange your will for His. As Christians, we're so quick to quote the text in Psalm 37:4-5 NKJV that says, "Delight yourself also in the Lord, And He shall give you the desires of your heart. Commit your way to the Lord, Trust also in Him, And He shall bring it to pass." What we fail to realize is that the only desires of your heart that God is going to give you are the ones that He placed there. You can only tap into that space with Him if you have surrendered and submitted your will to Him.

Even though it wasn't my own natural desire to work on this project, I had already given God my "yes" and it was time for me to hold up my end of the deal. He was coming to collect like a drug lord who had loaned me a brick of cocaine. Mans wanted His return on investment.

His instructions came fast and furious. It was time to write *Purpose-Driven Enterprise* and it was coming out in the Spring of 2022. I kept making excuses still. "Lord, three months isn't enough time to complete this assignment." He reinforced His stance. "But God, you wanted me to focus on The Milli Club and now I can't even open enrollment." His words came at me with fervor, "You will do My will." There was no point in arguing. It was a moot point.

I reluctantly started the work on the book in the hopes that my social media would escape bondage as soon as Tómas returned from vacation. He emailed me on January 20th with a voice of empathy and compassion. "Of course, I will work on this for you, Kendra," he replied gently. He said he would fix it and I stopped working on the book.

Weeks. Literal weeks went by before my social had its deliverance service. In the meantime, God was showing me that He wasn't playing. Without a real social media account, I got booked to be a keynote speaker in Los Angeles for a women's conference. Guess what topic my publicist had submitted for my application...

PURPOSE-DRIVEN ENTERPRISE!

I was sick. But I finally got the message. The audience over at @theekendrayhill didn't put any pressure on me to perform or teach them anything. They genuinely enjoyed my company. These were people who just wanted to hang out with me and stay up-to-date with whatever I had going on. Thursday, February 3rd was the day that the floodgates over Heaven opened and God let it rain. I logged back into my original account with the excitement of a child on Christmas morning - but that joy quickly dissolved. My @iamkendrayhill account was noisy. VERY noisy. There were people that I followed that I didn't even like. I had only reciprocated their follow for a follow. There were people that I had literally prayed out of my life who were popping up on my timeline. This side was way too busy and way too loud. Yearning for the peace that I had on my backup page, I started unfollowing, restricting, and blocking accounts. I needed an oasis if I was going to finish the book.

There are times in our lives when God really just needs you to silence the world around you. So many of us spend a lot of time doing other things like scrolling on TikTok, watching television, and gossiping on the phone. I told you back in Chapter 3 that God isn't going to compete with the noise of your life. Sometimes that noise is external and sometimes it's the war happening inside of yourself.

What's happening around you that is bringing you stress? What can be subtracted from the world around you to give you a more stress-free life? Dig deep - as you see my own environmental stress was hidden.

_____

_____

_____

_____

_____

_____

_____

What about internal distractions? What emotions do you need to deal
with? What is internally causing you stress? How can you navigate these
distractions?

_____

_____

_____

_____

_____

_____

_____

_____

19 [Lord], I need some discipline tonight

If you thought that exercise about shutting up the internal and external distractions was hard - haha. Prepare your heart. A big part of alignment is creating structure for yourself. I once read somewhere that children need structure and adults need freedom and I agree. If we really think about tapping into our God-given purpose, God is asking us to use our child-like faith in trusting Him. So yep - you're His kid and you need discipline.

<u>DISCIPLINE: verb \ ˈdi-sə-plən \</u>

to train or develop by instruction and exercise especially in self-control

Discipline was something that I struggled with as a young adult. When I was in my 20s, I had a hard time adapting to the idea of focusing and working hard to be successful. I skated through grade school. I was one of those annoying kids who didn't study, didn't have a tutor, and always got all A's. During my freshman year at Howard University, I got my first B in my academic career. It was from Dr. Livingston who taught sociology. I thought I could breeze through his class too, so I didn't study for tests. He made us do these stupid quizzes on Blackboard that were timed and had to be completed each week on a deadline. I bought the sociology textbook, but I can't remember a time when I opened it. I was working full-time on Capitol Hill and his class was the least of my concerns. Dr. Livingston was tough as nails though. He was an older Jamaican man who didn't take any crap from anyone. There wasn't a single excuse that was good enough to weasel out of taking his tests. If there was an emergency back home, he'd say, "Home wi tek care of itself." If you needed to attend a funeral, he'd reply, "Di dead wi bury di dead!" And if YOU died, you had better resurrect yourself and take that doggone test before you take your final resting place 6-feet under.

Although I literally cried about getting a B in his class, I still hadn't learned to be disciplined. I didn't learn the art of self-control until I was living in Sacramento. During that time (post-Guitar Hero playing madame), God had me on another level. Growing up in Holy Nation Baptist Church, we were the epitome of Baptist folks. The deacons smoked cigarettes on the backside of the building between Sunday service and Sunday School. Half of the choir was drunk less than an hour after leaving the parking lot. And don't even get me started on the affairs and fornication that was poppin' off. I hadn't learned anything about real spiritual discipline; only performative discipline that manifested as a "spirit of excellence."

My nine months in SacTown taught me how to fast. That's right - fast as in turning down my plate. I don't mean I was running fast. I mean I wasn't eating nothing for long periods of time. The very first fast I had to do was one of the hardest ones documented in the bible. I'm not talking about the Daniel fast where you're basically a vegan for 21 days (Daniel 1:8-14 and Daniel 10:12-13). I had to do the Esther fast which was no food and no water for 3 days (Esther 4:16).

#PAUSE

Scientifically speaking (shout out to my client AsapSCIENCE), the human body can survive without water for *about* 3 days. Because you are made up of about 60% water, you really need H2O in order to carry out essential functions of your body. Without it, you can overheat, get dehydrated, and become filled with poisonous toxins - oh yeah, and you can DIE! (Thanks for coming to my science-based Ted Talk).

God was pulling out the big guns. If I was ever going to be who I was supposed to be in Him, I would have to learn how to discipline myself. Considering food and water are necessities for survival, if I could train myself to go 3 days without them, somehow I would become mentally strong enough to make it through anything.

Chile, I might have blacked out in front of El Pollo Loco during a fast (I don't think so, but I really don't remember). I struggled through those 3 days. The first day was the worst - or so I thought. I couldn't think or really function at all. I felt like a zombie and the cotton mouth sensation was driving me up the wall. Day two brought about dry heaving and intense migraines. I couldn't even really sleep. I felt weak and tired, but couldn't find any rest. By the final day, I was just plotting what I was going to have at midnight when it was all over. I had actually missed the point of the fast.

God was swift and just in bringing another fast back around. About three weeks later, I was back at the Esther fast. This time, I went and studied the word concerning fasting. I found clear instructions in Matthew 6:16-18 NIV:

> "When you fast, do not look somber as the hypocrites do, for they disfigure their faces to show others they are fasting. Truly I tell you, they have received their reward in full. But when you fast, put oil on your head and wash your face, so that it will not be obvious to others that you are fasting, but only to your Father, who is unseen; and your Father, who sees what is done in secret, will reward you."

That made sense. I was telling everybody that I was on a fast and I was definitely moping around like a malnourished child in a Save the Children commercial (shout out to Lil Johnnie lol). So no pity parties. Got it. But outside of learning discipline, why did I need to fast? Acts 13:2-3 NIV revealed one of the main reasons:

> "While they were worshiping the Lord and fasting, the Holy Spirit said, "Set apart for me Barnabas and Saul for the work to which I have called them." So after they had fasted and prayed, they placed their hands on them and sent them off."

Okay, so I needed to fast so I could devote more time to prayer. Cool cool. Seemed wack to me lol. Isaiah 58:6 NIV came up:

> "Is not this the kind of fasting I have chosen: to loose the chains of injustice and untie the cords of the yoke, to set the oppressed free and break every yoke?"

Alrighty. So now I needed to be on my Tasha Cobbs-Leonard and "break every chain." This kinda made sense, especially when paired with Matthew 17:20-21 NKJV:

> "So Jesus said to them, "Because of your unbelief; for assuredly, I say to you, if you have faith as a mustard seed, you will say to this mountain, 'Move from here to there,' and it will move; and nothing will be impossible for you. However, this kind does not go out except by prayer and fasting."

Oh aiight. So we're increasing faith and bringing forth deliverance up in here! That was reason enough for me to really commit to fasting. As I continued to study, I quickly learned that fasting couldn't be used as spiritual blackmail against God. I wasn't supposed to fast to twist His arm… that would be taking advantage of His grace. God brought me back to the reason He told ME to fast - discipline.

I couldn't tell you how many fasts I went on while I was in Sacramento. Even well into 2018/2019, I was fasting regularly. If God said to go raw vegan for 30 days, I was eating fruits and veggies day and night like Kid Cudi. God said we're vegetarian for two weeks and I learned how to make scrambled tofu. Esther popped up every once in a while and I was down for 3 days with no problem.

June 2019 showed up and the discipline I had once surrendered to so easily became quite difficult. God told me that I was supposed to fast for 40 days without food. How? How I'm 'posed to do that? How??

Now let me remind you - this was a couple of months prior to me being exiled and fully stepping into my purpose. Don't skip over this lesson and this chapter thinking that it doesn't really apply to you. That scripture in Matthew about "this kind not going out but by prayer and fasting"? That scripture was in living color. Though there were dozens of things that contributed to me finding purpose, I really feel like this was the proverbial straw that broke the camel's back.

I spent the latter part of June and the greater part of July fasting with literally NO food. I wasn't taking vitamins and supplements. I didn't drink smoothies or sip broth. I literally only consumed water for 40 days. During this time, I still ran my business and did everything else I needed to do. Not only did I prove to myself that I could be extremely disciplined, but I also elevated to astronomical levels spiritually. Every morning, I would get up and begin the day with worship. Worship turned into prayer and prayer turned into battle. I had days where I would be singing new songs in tongues and my spiritual son Enoch would get the interpretation. There were nights when we prayed on the phone and Enoch and Pam would have open visions of the warfare in the second Heavens. It was wild! I'm grateful that I surrendered to that season even though it was challenging because it proved to me that I really can do all things through Christ who strengthens me.

Discipline becomes a major factor in your life once you fully tap into your purpose. It's discipline that has me up at 2:51 am writing this book. Discipline causes me to show up every week for The Milli Club even when I'm sick, tired, sick and tired, or sick of being tired. Discipline makes me fast and pray with a rebellious spiritual child who keeps repeating the same offenses. Discipline is a driving force in my life and this only came by prayer and fasting.

I want you to consider your own life. What are some experiences that you've had where you can see that God was trying to teach you discipline?

_____

_____

_____

_____

_____

_____

_____

Were these experiences before major transitions or shifts? When were they? What were the changes in your life that came immediately after?

_____

_____

_____

_____

_____

_____

_____

What are some ways that you can develop discipline? For some people, it's creating a morning routine and sticking to it. For others, it's committing to getting in the gym every day come hell or high water. How can you learn discipline in this season?

_____

_____

_____

_____

_____

_____

_____

20

Can We Go Deep, Deep, Deep, Deep?

Believe it or not, you're getting really close to discovering your purpose (if you haven't already). This journey has probably felt like a bunch of meandering and wandering through a fairytale forest waiting on the big bad wolf or a witch to jump out and attack you. No attacks here, but I'm sure you're whooped. I AM.

Let's do an easy exercise as a "cool down" as we get ready to fully write out our purpose statement and get into making this schmoney. I want you to think about your own life. We've already covered a lot of your life from pain and passions to experiences and relationships. You're going to need to pull from your former exercises to dig into this next section.

What are some indicators you've noticed in your own life when you were aligned?

_____

_____

_____

_____

_____

_____

_____

_____

When I am properly aligned with God's will and timing for my life, it's paradise. Literally. Blue skies. Sunshine. Wind blowing through my hair. Paradise. At least that's how it feels. My mony is right. My mind is right. My life feels peaceful and I can sense that I am in the right place at the right time. I'm not burnt out or stressed about anything or anyone. And I know that I know that I'm aligned when I have my blockers on and I'm not paying attention to what anyone else is doing. That's a HUGE indicator for me. When I'm just doing my thing without being concerned about people on the internet, I know I'm in my flow.

What are some indicators you've experienced when you were NOT aligned?

_____

_____

_____

_____

_____

_____

_____

_____

I know for me personally that I am out of alignment when I start feeling frustrated with my life. Back in 2021 I started spiraling. I remember having a conversation with Tre where I was telling him that I didn't even know what brought me joy anymore. I felt frustrated and stressed out every single day. It wasn't like my business was failing or I was losing money or anything like that. I legit just felt sorrow in my spirit. When I really stepped back and analyzed what was happening, I realized that God was nudging me to start managing talent in a larger capacity. Specifically, that I was supposed to start managing Black female influencers. I surrendered to the leading of the Holy Spirit and the rest is history.

Alignment isn't just about being in tune with where you should be in life, but it also encompasses discipline. In the chart below, I want you to write out your ideal daily routine. You may not be functioning in this routine right now, and that's okay. You need to outline what your basic routine would look like in a perfect world.

6 AM	
7AM	
8AM	
9AM	
10AM	
11 AM	
12 PM	
1 PM	
2 PM	
3 PM	
4 PM	
5 PM	
6 PM	
7 PM	
8 PM	
9 PM	
10 PM	

My own routine has changed so much over the last few years. When I was living in Canada in 2020, I was getting up at 5:00 am so I could have time for myself before going into my client's office at 9:00 am. I actually had plans for a podcast called *5AM in Toronto* because I would get up and have these deep conversations with God that I felt others could also learn from. As soon as I moved back to the States, I dropped that early morning habit.

My routine now is a bit more fluid, but I have a few basic parameters. I only take meetings Tuesday - Thursday between 11:00 am - 4:00 pm.

I use my Monday as an administrative day and my Friday as a day for creativity. I try to get up two hours before my first meeting of the day so I have time to pray, do my morning pages, have breakfast and handle any grooming that I need to do. When I finish with my meetings, I usually have a snack and take a nap. After a brief rest, I get up, have dinner, teach classes and get some work done before heading to bed at about 2-3:00 am. I function really well on about four hours of sleep.

What's stopping you from having your ideal routine?

_____

_____

_____

_____

_____

_____

_____

Before we get into this next question, I want you to assess everything that you've written in this book so far. You've dealt with your past and any hidden things, discovered your Golden Spoon, and considered your life's experiences. So, what do you feel most led to do with your life RIGHT NOW?

_____

_____

_____

_____

_____

_____

Write the [Purpose].
Make it Plain.

Finally, the chapter you've been waiting for - let's write your purpose statement!

When I wrote out my purpose statement in the comments section of my YouTube video, multiple things happened. For one, it finally felt real. I didn't plan on writing it out like that, but the words flowed from my brain to my fingertips like honey. It didn't feel coerced or forced. It felt like this was what I was really meant to do. Secondly, it lifted a huge weight off of my shoulders. I had been battling with my purpose for about 7 years. I would get to a place in my life where I was really happy and content and then boom! I'd get hit with the reality that I still didn't have purpose or direction in my life.

Being able to write out my purpose statement with clarity has given me so much peace, but it also makes decision-making easy. I have always been a bit indecisive. I was the kind of person who wanted to weigh out every outcome with pros and cons lists, Venn diagrams, line graphs, and everything in between. Settling on my purpose makes it easy to make plans and decisions. If an opportunity clearly aligns with my purpose, then I do it. If it doesn't, then I trash it.

Finding my purpose has also helped me stop being so future-focused. I was the kind of person who wanted to map out my 10-year plan with exact dates, times, and weather predictions (I was crazy lol). Accepting and leaning into my purpose has allowed me to actually enjoy my life. I'm literally living the life of my dreams.

But let's take a look at the importance of writing this thing out. A familiar passage of scripture is found in Habakkuk 2:2-3 AMP: "Then the Lord answered me and said, "Write the vision and engrave it plainly on [clay] tablets so that the one who reads it will run. "For the vision is yet for the appointed [future] time it hurries toward the goal [of fulfillment]; it will not fail. Even though it delays, wait [patiently] for it, Because it will certainly come; it will not delay."

Whew! SO much to unpack here. Like...I could literally do a whole 4-week bible study on these two verses alone but in the interest of time and space, I will share the Cliff Notes version lol. A couple of things to accept immediately:

1. Whatever vision God has given you was created for a specific point and time. There's a date on it. Now...you may not know the date lol, but there IS a date.

2. Even if your purpose or the manifestation of your purpose SEEMS slow, be patient and wait on God. It will be fulfilled. Periodt.

<u>SEEMS: verb \ ˈsēm \</u>

to give the impression of being

The word "seems" literally means that it appears to be - appears to feel - gives the appearance of. Basically...it ain't the truth. We FEEL like the fulfillment of purpose is delayed. We FEEL like we're behind schedule. We FEEL like we aren't seeing the manifestation of God's promises. We FEEL like we're lost. Feelings are fickle. Jeremiah 17:9 KJV makes it so clear, "The heart is deceitful above all things, and desperately wicked: who can know it?" Chile, nobody can know it but God, because the fact is that our feelings lead us astray ALL. THE. TIME.

But the BIGGER point I want to make with this text is that your God-given purpose isn't just for you. This is why God tells the prophet Habakkuk to "write the vision and make it plain". Whatever it is that God has revealed to you about your purpose isn't even about you (sorry, not sorry).

Forgive me while I get in my old preacher bag lol (read: alliteration). So when God gives us vision, here's what we have to do with it:

SEE IT

Back up in verse 1, Habakkuk says that he "will watch to see what he [God] will say unto me". You have to open yourself up to accept what it is that God wants to show you. It's only through dedicated time and a willing vessel that the Holy Spirit can reveal the heart of God towards you. So you position yourself to hear from God by waiting and watching to see what He has to say.

After you've been through all of the other exercises in the book, I want you to ask God what He is saying to you concerning your purpose. Jot it down here.

_____

_____

_____

_____

_____

_____

_____

_____

SHARE IT

God tells Habakkuk to "write the vision". So it wasn't just for him to see and hold on to. God revealed what He revealed to Habakkuk so that he could share the word with the kingdom of Judah. This is why building your own tribe is so important. You need people around you that you can share your God-given vision with.

Right now, who are the trusted people in your circle? Who can you share your purpose journey with? Don't feel pressured to fill in all of these lines. You only need one person, tbh.

_____

_____

_____

_____

_____

_____

_____

SEAL IT

God didn't just tell Habakkuk to write it on a piece of paper (which probably would've been a scroll back then). He told him to write it on tablets. That means that he had to engrave it and make it permanent. In the same way, God wants us to seal and confirm the word that He gave us. There's no reason to second guess or doubt or need five million confirmations (*coughs* Kendra!). What He says is what He means and He's so sure of it that He wants you to make a permanent declaration about it.

Brainstorm ways you can share your purpose in a more public way. I wrote mine in the comments section of my YouTube video and now I've written a whole book that highlights my purpose over and over. How can you share your God-given purpose with your audience?

_____

_____

_____

_____

_____

_____

_____

_____

SIMPLIFY IT

"Make it plain". OK, so boom. So often, we try to overcomplicate what God has shared with us. What does that sound like? "I don't have enough followers to do XYZ." Or, "I'm not really ready because I don't think I'm an expert." Or, "I need to wait because if you want me to do X then I need to do Y&Z too." We make excuses when God is trying to make it plain. Just do what He said, when He said it, the way He said it. We should move in a way that allows us and those working with us to gain insight and make moves (i.e. run).

Right here, right now, I want you to fill in the blank.

My God-given purpose is to _____

If you feel stuck, take a break. This sentence should come to you easily. Also, it's not necessarily your final purpose statement. It's just brain vomit that you need to get out of your head and onto paper. We'll revisit this in a moment.

SPEAK IT

When you are preparing to fully walk in the purpose that God has given you, you have to keep speaking it. Keeping your purpose in front of you is so important to the success of your business. Your full purpose itself will speak when it's time, so while you're waiting on it to do that, you speak it with confidence until it happens.

I'm gonna make this one easy for you. Shoot me a DM at instagram.com/iamkendrayhill or an email at heyhey@kendrascalemybusiness.com with what you feel your purpose is. Use me as practice. It's a safe place where you can share your purpose and also get feedback without judgment.

In the words of Kanye West, "It's what you all been waiting for, ain't it? What people pay paper for, ain't it?" Follow the prompts to develop your final God-given purpose statement.

Here's mine again for reference:

> My purpose is to help motivate and inspire others to align themselves with God's plan for their lives.

Here's your purpose formula. If you need more help or ideas, use the exercise below to solidify your words:

My purpose is to _____ *(service-based verb)*
_____ *(who)*

_____ *(do what?).*

Circle a service-based verb:

Administer	Cooperate	Intervene
Advocate	Counsel	Listen
Aide	Demonstrate	Motivate
Alleviate	Diagnose	Prevent
Answer	Direct	Provide
Arrange	Educate	Refer
Assess	Encourage	Relieve
Assist	Ensure	Represent
Attend to	Expedite	Resolve
Benefit	Facilitate	Serve
Clarify	Further	Support
Coach	Give	Treat
Collaborate	Guide	Volunteer
Contribute	Help	

Choose a group of people (these are just a few different groups - feel free to add your own):

Artists	Entrepreneurs	Performers
Athletes	Expats	Singers
Businessowners	Husbands	Soldiers
Children	Men	Students
Creatives	Musicians	Teachers
Dancers	Others	Tourists
Directors	Parents	Wives
Employees	People	Women

Let's take it a step further now. Add an adjective to describe your group of people:

My purpose is to _____ (service-based verb) _____ (adjective)

_____ (who) _____ _____ (do what?).

Based on this exercise, I would shift my statement around a bit. Here's my revision:

My purpose is to motivate and inspire faith-based entrepreneurs to align themselves with God's plan for their lives.

Not only did I omit "help" but I also niched down to faith-based entrepreneurs. Most likely you bought this book because you're a faith-based business owner (or you just know and love me - thank you).

Use this space to write your statement with your niched down target audience:

_____

_____

_____

_____

NOW, *ting*, we're going to add to this right now but know that this next part will change multiple times throughout your life. We're just going to fill in the blanks now with what is current.

My purpose is to _____ (service-based verb) _____ (adjective)

_____ (who) _____ _____ (do what?)

through _____
(how do you do this?)

As a reference, here is my new statement:

> My purpose is to motivate and inspire faith-based entrepreneurs to align themselves with God's plan for their lives through training, advisory, and hands-on implementation of spiritual principles.

Dig deep and consider how you help your audience do whatever it is you're supposed to help them do. This may not come to you immediately, but give yourself some time to discover what fits best here. Revisit some of your writings about times when you felt like your best self. Your Golden Spoon may apply here as well.

Now, take this space to write out your complete statement:

_____

_____

_____

_____

_____

_____

THAT'S IT! You've found purpose! It may seem very simple, but honestly, purpose IS simple. What makes purpose complicated is the various manifestations it takes over time. Before we move past this, let's take a moment to reflect. Looking at your purpose statement, how does it make you feel?

_____

_____

_____

_____

_____

_____

Had you already been operating in your purpose all along?

_____

_____

_____

_____

_____

_____

_____

What are you most looking forward to now?

_____

_____

_____

_____

_____

_____

_____

_____

[Vision] So Big.
Lawd Hammercy!

Wow. We've accomplished so much together and we're really just getting started. The rest of this book will guide you through monetizing your purpose in big tangible ways. But first - a story!

Once I wrote my purpose statement on YouTube, I felt limited. Was I only allowed to fulfill my purpose as a business consultant? Is that why God needed me to come back to consulting? What if I wanted to do or be something else? The questions were racing around in my head like glitter in a tornado. God's voice grounded me. "Your purpose doesn't change. The dispensation does."

DISPENSATION: noun \ ˌdi-spən-ˈsā-shən\

an appointment, arrangement, or favor, as by God.

Remember that lesson on assignments? We're back. Bing bong! God gives us different assignments but our core purpose remains the same. When I was a stylist, my purpose was to align people with God's plan. When I was a television producer, my purpose was to align people with God's plan. When I was a brand manager, my purpose was to align people with God's plan. And guess what? As a business consultant, my purpose is to align people with God's plan.

The purpose doesn't change. The dispensation does (over time).

So if you're concerned about being limited by your purpose statement, let it go. You'll find that God will consistently use you to fulfill your purpose in whatever role you're in. The key is to stay close enough to Him that you can hear when there's a shift coming. God will speak to you and let you know that a change is on the horizon. You may not get details immediately, but eventually, you'll understand why the shift is happening.

What you have to come to terms with is this: God's plan for you is so big that it can't be contained by one job, one assignment, or one project. Limiting yourself to one thing for the rest of your life actually limits God and His ability to use you as He sees fit. The best thing you can do is surrender fully to Him and allow yourself to be molded and used as a vessel of His Holy Ghost power.

Now that your purpose statement is clear, let's reflect a bit:

Consider your current career. Is it in alignment with your purpose? Why or why not?

_____

_____

_____

_____

_____

_____

Pinpoint three times in your life where your purpose has shown up.

First Instance.

_____

_____

_____

_____

_____

_____

_____

Second Instance.

_____

_____

_____

_____

_____

_____

Third Instance.

_____

_____

_____

_____

_____

_____

For me, there are wayyyyyy more than three instances where my purpose has shown up in living color, but here are my top three:

1. The birth of Prophetess Kendra Y. Hill Ministries - No doubt, this is an easy application of my God-given purpose. During this season, I was traveling the world preaching and teaching

the Gospel plus conducting deliverance services, and acting as an interim pastor in multiple ministries. I worked in groups and one-on-one to get folks aligned with God's plan for them.

2. Launching Kendra, Scale My Business - Aside from the fact that this purpose moment brought so many of God's promises for me to fruition, my time as a business consultant has allowed me to minister to people outside of the church. Through this business, God has trusted me to share my faith with people who were atheists, agnostics, and even Scientologists.

3. Writing *Purpose-Driven Enterprise* - I don't know if I've ever felt so aligned in my life. Although the writing of this book has come with its own warfare (chile, there was a point where I was sick for a whole week with no explanation), I've never felt so much peace and assurance that I was doing the right thing.

Revisit your journal entries in chapter 7 where you wrote about being your best self. Now that you know your purpose, were you operating in purpose when you were your best self? How does being your best self correlate with your purpose statement?

_____

_____

_____

_____

_____

_____

23 I Will Open Up My Heart...

There's a harsh reality that I've been trying to avoid but I can't anymore. If you've gotten this far and you still feel lost or like you don't know if your purpose statement is fitting, then keep reading...

I lived in Dallas for about 3 years (from 2015 to 2018). During that time I stayed everywhere from a mansion in Highland Park to an apartment in Arlington and an extended stay in Grand Prairie. While I was staying in the rundown motel, I saw God in unimaginable ways. From writing my first book, *Suffer Not a Witch to Live* to receiving open prophetic visions for the first time, Budget Suites was an incubator for my prophetic gift.

There came a time when God would have me go on these late-night drives to commune with Him. The 400-square-foot suite that I shared with my mom wasn't enough space for me to connect with Him like I needed to. The drives started as short-distance jaunts to the McDonald's down the road. The 3-minute drive was nothing compared to the 26-minute jaunt to Wal-Mart that later became my routine route.

I was very familiar with the Wal-Mart in Bedford, Texas. It was right next door to Daystar Television Network where the first show I ever produced was aired. Sitting in the nearly vacant parking lot after midnight had become my norm. I would usually sit and listen to worship music, pray and meditate. Sometimes I sat there for twenty minutes and sometimes it took two hours, but I knew I couldn't leave until God gave me instructions.

One night in particular, I was on the phone with Janine (my then-BFF) and my apostle Adrienne. We were talking about everything from church services we had recently attended to deep revelation. I parked in my usual spot under an old parking lot light. As Janine and Adrienne were rambling on about some new discovery in the book of Luke, I turned on some music. I was playing some of my favorite gospel songs from Hezekiah Walker, Donald Lawrence, and Richard Smallwood. I put my head back on the headrest and closed my eyes I saw myself standing on a stage in the middle of a huge arena. I had on a white skirt suit with a peplum jacket. My hair was straight and long with a middle part framing my face. Though I couldn't hear myself, I could tell that the spirit had broken out in the building and I was encouraging everyone to push in even more. Some people were swaying and crying while others were shouting and dancing. It was a real Azusa Revival experience.

Somehow I came back to myself and heard "Total Praise" fade away and a familiar song from Walter Hawkins began playing in the background. As Tremaine Hawkins sang, "When I think about...," I drifted back into the open vision of the arena, except this time, there was a funeral service. Many were weeping as "Jesus Christ is the Way" was being sung by a small group of anointed singers. People were kneeling down at the altar near the casket praying and surrendering to God. I scanned the crowd for familiar faces when I landed on Nixon and Adrienne standing in the area with the preachers on the stage. Seeing Nixon's bloodshot eyes, I grew anxious and concerned. My eyes fell to the casket and I saw what I dreaded most. There I was in my white peplum suit with my eyes closed looking as though I was sleeping in the most peaceful dream. It was my own funeral.

In real life, tears began to pour out of my eyes like a raging waterfall. For some reason, my eyes felt like they were cemented together with gorilla glue. I couldn't pull myself out of the vision. "I will open up my heart to everyone I see. AND SAYYYYYYYYYYYYY...." I looked around the arena as the ensemble brought the song to a close with a dramatic flair, holding the note for what felt like an eternity. The cries and shouts of the audience roared around the arena so much that it shook the ground we were standing on. "Jesus Christ is the way." The singers finished and exited the stage as the musicians continued to play a soft reprise. Nixon stepped toward the podium in the middle of the stage and his ring-lad-ened left hand grabbed the microphone. My eyes flew open.

I was still inconsolable as I came back to my natural self. Seeing myself in a casket was soul-stirring in every way imaginable. Still sobbing and trying to catch my breath, I heard Janine ask what happened. Adrienne calmly whispered, "She just died to her own understanding."

Weeks passed before Adrienne and I discussed that night but what was incredibly clear was that there was a change in me. When my apostle and I finally had a conversation about my funeral, she explained to me that in order to go where God was taking me and in order to fully receive and walk in my purpose, I had to stop leaning on my own understanding (Proverbs 3:5-6). If I wanted to be used for His purpose, I had to allow God to make my name great which meant that I had to stop relying on my own knowledge.

If you still feel like you don't know what to do or you aren't clear on your God-given purpose, then I challenge you to spiritually die to your own understanding. That process may not be as ceremonious or dramatic as mine was, but if you would surrender and submit your will to God and ask Him to help you stop questioning Him and His leading, I guarantee you that He will meet you where you are.

Right now, I want you to take a moment and ask God to show you where your trepidation lies. Are you being too analytical or logical? Are you doubting yourself? Maybe you're afraid of what happens when you fully commit to His way. Whatever it is, I want you to articulate it out loud to Him and wait on Him to respond. Jot down what He says and ask Him to show you how to be delivered from that hindrance.

_____

_____

_____

_____

Bills, Bills, Bills

You're ready to go to the next part of this process: monetizing. But first, let's talk about your money mindset.

When it comes to using our purpose in business, we have to change the way we view jobs, careers, money, etc. We work to pay our bills, have fun with the extra, and are often satisfied with stability. But when you're aligned with your purpose, you realize that your main goal should be fulfilling your purpose, and the work you do should be a means to achieving your purpose. You have to be okay with changing careers at times if your current role isn't on the path to achieving your purpose - and you have to be okay with not making money when you first start walking in purpose.

You already know how I was feeling about going back into business consulting as a profession. God literally had to put me in exile to get me to surrender and submit (chile, don't be like me). But I had to come to terms with the fact that God was moving me from a career/job-based mindset into a purpose mindset. I had to trust Him in that process. I was worried about the wrong things; I was ultimately concerned that I wouldn't be able to make good money as a consultant (which is crazy because I could obviously make more money as a consultant than as a stylist). The deeper I dug into my situation, the more I realized that I had money mindset issues. How could God bless me the way He wanted to when I had a poor attitude towards money?

A lot of people grew up in low-income environments (311 Robeson) or have made poor financial decisions (*coughs* Bank of America credit cards at 18 smh). Because of that, your mindset may be focused on merely surviving. Survival mode puts you in a space where you're actual-ly afraid of taking risks that may result in any type of loss. This mentality is a supersized combo meal at your least favorite fast-food franchise. Your #6 meal is "the thought that you have to work one job for the rest of your life and climb the corporate ladder." It comes with a side of "a million streams of income" and a large "lack of knowledge about finances."

The money mindset is all about making that mental shift by transforming your relationship with money. This doesn't mean that all you should think about is money. It's about creating a relationship with money that allows you to view it as something you:

- deserve.

- can make in your sleep.

- know is not finite.

- can spend without guilt.

- can save efficiently.

Walking in purpose in your business takes trusting that as you fulfill God's plan, the money will follow. It's easy to get stuck somewhere for the pay-check, but how much more fulfilled could we be if we changed the lens we use to view our work life?

If you find more of your time and energy is focused on increasing your salary or getting a new job title versus your impact in a role, then you may be suffering from a poverty or career mindset. It's absolutely OKAY to want to make more money in your business or want to move up in your company, especially if you are feeling passionate, but you have to take a pause and consider the driving force. Is it the compensation or the impact you could have in that position?

Your best bet at getting further in the business world is focusing on your purpose. When working to fulfill that, your productivity, happiness, and general satisfaction go wayyy up. This is when the money starts falling in

your lap! You start to see promotions and raises a lot quicker, you make
more sales, and you generally feel good about going to work every day.

187

BILLS, BILLS, BILLS

LET'S GO BACK IN TIME...AGAIN.

Looking back over your life, what are the situations or experiences that
may have impacted your relationship with money? Some of these things
could be:

- Having immigrant parents/being an immigrant

- Watching parents live paycheck to paycheck

- Eating cheap meals (ramen, beanies and weenies, air/mus-
tard/mayo sandwiches)

- Not having money for school lunch or clothes

Take a moment below to reflect.

_____

_____

_____

_____

_____

_____

_____

_____

How old were you when you first remember money as a concept? What
do you remember learning about it? What did it mean to you?

_____

_____

_____

187

_____

_____

_____

_____

_____

Is there a time that you were ever without? What was that incident? How did it make you feel?

_____

_____

_____

_____

_____

_____

_____

_____

Imagine you have to make a big purchase TODAY- say a house or a car. How does this make you feel? Why?

_____

_____

_____

_____

_____

_____

_____

_____

Do you feel worthy of this new house or car? Why or why not?

_____

_____

_____

_____

_____

_____

_____

How do you act around money? Are you comfortable around wealth? What does that look like?

_____

_____

_____

_____

_____

_____

_____

_____

How are you about asking for what you are worth? Is it hard? Are you comfortable requesting your rate/pricing?

_____

_____

_____

_____

_____

_____

_____

_____

Let's tackle some current mental blocks when it comes to money. Be honest and transparent as you fill in the three blanks below:

1. I cannot generate wealth today because _____

   _____

   _____

2. I could only become a millionaire if _____

   _____

   _____

3. When it comes to making money, I don't know how to _____

   _____

   _____

Were you surprised by any of these answers? Do you see how your money mindset impacts your ability to monetize your purpose?

_____

_____

_____

_____

_____

_____

_____

Up [Shift's] Creek

I want to give you practical steps that you can take to change your money mindset QUICKLY. So I'm cutting the fluff and erasing the stories. Push through this chapter NOW so we can start monetizing your purpose in the next one. Changing your mindset actually becomes very easy when you start with the little things.

LEARNING

The best way to get comfortable with money is to learn about it. This doesn't mean you need to become a financial expert or a social media money guru who talks about money but doesn't actually make any (okay...sorry). But learn about things like credit or even just simple budgeting. Financial literacy will help you plan. Sit down and figure out what income you have coming in and what your expenses REALLY are. Then make a budget and go from there! Don't forget to set aside a little extra "treat yourself" coins!

It's perfectly fine to be forever learning - even I am. Right now, I'm on my NFT flow learning how I can make non-fungible tokens a part of my assets that I can pass on to my children. We are taught a LOT of things in school, but unfortunately, financial literacy isn't one of them. Take your time learning and be patient with yourself. You may be unlearning old habits and developing new ones. Educate yourself and extend grace.

FACE YOUR FEARS

The survival mindset often creates fear - fear of spending money, fear of saving money, and fear of not having enough of it. That same fear tells us that if we take risks, we will either spend too much money or not make enough to sustain the lifestyle we want. The moment we think of that, some of us drop out! But you CANNOT let that be the reason you dodge the things that are meant for you. Don't get caught up in the cycle.

What are you actually afraid of when it comes to money?

_____

_____

_____

_____

_____

_____

_____

Of the things you wrote, which are actual vs. just a feeling?

_____

_____

_____

_____

_____

_____

_____

STOP OBSESSING

Unpopular opinion, but STOP checking your bank account. Now, of course, there are times it's necessary but don't let it take over. There are people who check their accounts every time they spend a dime. There are other people who go see how much money they have just to spend it. Take a breath and release it! Trust your budgeting plan and check in weekly, but don't allow this habit to take over. If you are constantly focused on the money you have, you'll never be able to focus on more money coming IN!

Currently, I check my account (when)…

_____

_____

_____

_____

_____

_____

_____

_____

Moving forward I will only check my account....

1. _____

2. _____

FORGIVE YOURSELF

Forgive money decisions you made in your past. It's easy to get worked up thinking about the money we shouldn't have spent, or money we spent in a way that didn't make us feel good. Get over it and trust that God has GOT YOU!

Okay I lied…one story.

I was that 18-year-old who had the Bank of America credit card that put me in debt with a credit score of 520. First of all, who allows CHILDREN (because 18 is still a childish age) to borrow so much money??? Oh yeah... Sallie Mae, Navient, etc. Anyway, I had a card that I used to buy all of the new clothes that I needed every week for nights in the club. I was dating a guy named Kareem who was amazing - until he wasn't (woosah...this story is not about a cheating, conniving negro who broke my little heart). He was a 23-year-old graduate of Yale who worked for Nasdaq, lived in a condo in Georgetown, and drove a Benz. He and his friends got together and opened a pretty dope nightclub in Chinatown called Faces.

At 18, none of my friends were able to get into 21+ clubs and we definitely weren't able to drink while we were out. Well, Kareem made sure that me and my homegirls were VIP with bottle service every week at Faces. I took Aryana and Amal when I wanted to sit pretty, Tiffany and Janelle when I wanted to unwind and Oreo and Andrea when I wanted to turn up. Regardless of who I brought, we always had a good time, but a good time was only guaranteed if I visited Pentagon City first.

Pentagon City was THEE mall when I was at Howard. If you needed something cute to wear to the club, work, or anywhere in-between, you could definitely find it at one of the 164 stores. From Nordstrom and Macy's to Forever XXI and Aldo, this mall had everything you needed. I spent all of my little internship money on outfits and when that wasn't enough, I marched myself up Georgia Avenue to Bank of America to apply for a credit card. I was instantly approved with a credit limit of $500 (which was big money to me then lol).

I don't even think the sun set before that mug was maxed out. I used it to buy two dresses at Nordstrom and Auntie Ann's pretzels for whoever was with me. I had no idea what financial literacy OR fiscal responsibility was. I did, however, know how to misappropriate funds and spend irresponsible amounts of money to make a good impression.

That was just the first of many money mistakes I made while living in DC. I also got an apartment that was more than half of my income so I could stunt on my peers. I went into debt buying those Gucci sunglasses and Louboutin sneakers for Bryson (that I ended up throwing out into the snow anyway). I also ended up with that subsequent eviction on my credit when I left Bryson.

As a mature adult who was starting over in California, I had to forgive myself for the mistakes of my past. Though I was still reaping the consequences of my actions years later, I had educated myself on basic money management and I was ready to start over.

What are some financial mistakes you've made in the past that may still be impacting you right now?

_____

_____

_____

_____

_____

_____

_____

_____

Let's move past these mistakes. Here are some affirmations that I said daily until I really started believing them:

- I am no longer the mistakes of my past.

- My poor financial planning of yesterday does not dictate my positive decision-making for tomorrow.

- I will use my budget and plan to move forward in positivity when it comes to money.

- From now on, I only think of money with joy, knowing that every day is an opportunity to live in abundance.

CAN YOU SAVE?

Learn to stop spending all the money you have. It's important to save money passively. Stay in for the night and let that extra $20 become $200. I really recommend that you make it easy by diversifying your accounts. When my direct deposit hits, 20% of it goes into another account that accrues interest over time. I tuck away the money before I can even see it and make plans for it.

Make a commitment right now to save some money. How much money do you want to save over the next 3 months?

$_____

How will you do this easily?

_____

_____

_____

_____

_____

_____

_____

_____

STOP "DESERVING"

Don't treat money as a reward. You don't have to "deserve" everything. You deserve things because you are a living, breathing, human who is a contributing member of society. While it can be nice to reward yourself with exuberance every once in a while, you should treat yourself to simple things regularly.

What's one thing you can treat yourself to over the next 3 months WHILE you save money?

FALLING OUT OF AGREEMENT WITH POVERTY

We've come this far in the lesson without being TOO directly connected to faith and spirituality, but I don't know how to do anything (especially generate wealth and abundance) without God's help.

I have spent a great deal of time praying and fasting to break the curse of poverty off of my bloodline. These are notes from my journals dating back to 2014 when I focused on my future and the wealth of my children's children:

Lord, I trust You to be my provider.

I destroy all assignments of the enemy against my finances in the name of Jesus.

I break all curses of lack, poverty, and debt.

I renounce every vow and pledge to poverty rooted in religious error, ignorance, and bloodline issues in the name of Jesus.

I break every operation of poverty and lack assigned against my life and I renounce every support system at work in my mind.

I renounce all greed, covetousness, and lust for things associated with poverty.

Lord, allow good stewardship to be my portion.

Lord, forgive me for any and all negligence concerning the seed and finances you've put in my hands.

I loose myself from all ignorance and knowledge blocking strongholds concerning prosperity and financial increase.

I renounce every mentality and mindset I've inherited that's rooted in mediocrity and poverty.

As I meditate on the word day and night, I know that whatever I do prospers. (Psalm 1:3)

God has given me the power to create wealth. (Deuteronomy 8:18)

Lord, teach me to profit, and lead me in the way I should go. (Isaiah 48:17)

I trust that my home will be full and overflowing. (Psalm 144:13-14)

I receive the blessing of Abraham on my life and family line. (Genesis 12:1-3)

I am Your servant, Lord. Prosper me. (Nehemiah 2:20)

I live in the prosperity of the King. (Jeremiah 23:5)

Wealth and riches are in my house. (Psalm 112:1-3)

The blessing of the Lord makes me rich and adds no sorrow. (Proverbs 10:22)

Lord, help me to walk right before you and leave an inheritance for my children's children when I leave this earthly vessel. (Proverbs 13:22)

25 Then I'm a Give The Business To You

This chapter is meant to get you thinking about purpose in business. Our labor has to be about more than just our next paycheck. Again, this goes back to our purpose being about our impact, not just our personal aspirations. So, what can we be doing during our 40+ hours of work every week to make sure we fulfill our purpose?

When I took the position in Congressman Farr's office, I was bright-eyed and bushy-tailed with aspirations to one day have a congressional office with my name on it. Armed with the dream that Rev. Linda fit me with, I took Capitol Hill by storm in the hopes of being a politician who would change the world. The job of my dreams quickly became the slaveship of my nightmares as I learned more about appropriations, filibusters, and congressional back-scratching. One Congressman who was friends with another would coerce them to sign their bill to get it on the floor for votes. The work that was happening in the hallowed halls of Congress was all about performing favors for your political cronies. The constituents didn't matter as much as I thought they should and I quickly became disenchanted with the work in Washington.

Let me be clear: this is nothing against Congressman Farr. He was dope and genuinely cared about his constituents. But I paid attention to everyone. A lot of my colleagues worked for sneaky, shiesty, shady Senators and Congressmen who would do anything to pad their pockets. You have to remember, this was during the reign of Anthony Weiner's sexcapades, Sarah Palin's "bridge to nowhere" blunder, and John

Edward's illegitimate child. It was the wild wild west as we prepared to inaugurate President Barack Obama. I knew I couldn't stay in a legislative office for much longer. I actually resigned from my position without another job lined up. Though money should've been a motivator, I was a 21-year-old with the hustle of my cocaine-smuggling man Bryson - I would find another job.

Think of a time when you worked in a role you weren't satisfied with. What were some signs that you needed to leave?

_____

_____

_____

_____

_____

_____

_____

Were there any barriers that stopped you from leaving?

_____

_____

_____

_____

_____

_____

_____

_____

What did you do to eliminate those barriers?

_____

_____

_____

_____

_____

_____

What are your current career goals?

_____

_____

_____

_____

_____

_____

_____

Are you working towards your purpose in your current role?

_____

_____

_____

_____

_____

_____

_____

_____

What are some roles you could be in to help you fulfill your purpose?

_____

_____

_____

_____

_____

_____

_____

If you could be anything you wanted, what would you be?

_____

_____

_____

_____

_____

_____

_____

If you haven't already, would you open your own business to help drive your purpose? What would your business be, and how would you overall be impactful?

If you're already a business owner, does your business drive your purpose? What are you doing that is impactful?

_____

_____

_____

_____

_____

_____

_____

26 Mo' Money, [No] Problems

When it comes to monetizing your purpose, there are some steps you need to take to get there. You also need to remember that it usually doesn't happen overnight. You have to be prepared to make sacrifices including your time, your energy, and often your money. You might have to leave your current job or start a new business to make it happen. TRUST that God has your back. He made you to fulfill this purpose, and will support your venture to get there!

People often think that making $6 million dollars in 2 years is an example of my overnight success. Let me go ahead and set the record straight: NOTHING about what I have or what I have done has been an overnight success. By now, you know more about what I've been through than some people who have known me for decades. Nothing in this life has been easy for me.

You have to remember that I ran IASA Consulting Group for 6 years. During that time, I learned how to do a trillion things, including how to build websites, make graphics, design layouts, direct art, keep financial records, do business taxes, conduct business in foreign territories, hire a team, manage employees, create a company culture, handle lawsuits, and everything else. After 6 years of running a business with 3 offices, 18 full-time employees, and 5 interns, I hit burnout - HARD. I was over it and completely disengaged. Then I started the styling business and ran that for about 2 to 2.5 years. So when I started Kendra, Scale My Business, I had been a business owner for 9 years. Nothing about that is overnight. It took me 9 years to become a multi-millionaire with a THRIVING business. So just remember that God will bless it when it's time - and that time usually comes when you're whole, mature, complete, and walking in your calling.

Let's revisit our discussion from chapter 4 about passions. This is probably the best route to monetizing your purpose. If you can do something you are passionate about, you are that much more likely to succeed. You are also more likely to put in the extra time, push through hard times, and inspire more people around you.

If you are currently in a position where you have a business and you are struggling to monetize, you might find that you actually aren't aligned with your purpose. That's not the ONLY reason why. You could be inconsistent or lazy OR it could be a season of preparation.

SN: when God is ready to elevate you, you'll often feel a temporary moment of stagnation. It's almost as if you hit a sudden brick wall. That's a good sign that God is putting you into an incubation season of preparation.

<u>INCUBATE: verb \ ˈiŋ-kyə-ˌbāt \</u>

to cause or aid the development of

It's God's desire to develop you fully before He sends you out into the world. The worst thing that can happen to you is that you become overexposed while you're underdeveloped. Think about it like old film photography. Exposing the film to light too soon ruins the image. To preserve and protect your reputation and image, God usually puts you in a dark place so you can fully mature and develop. It's normal.

You could have already been through your preparation season and still not be seeing a financial kickback to your purpose-driven enterprise. Don't trip. Here are some key steps you can take to make sure you monetize on your purpose:

STEP ONE: BE CLEAR ABOUT YOUR PURPOSE AND PASSIONS

We've done a lot of self-assessments over the course of this journey together. There's a really good chance that you aren't even the same person right now as you were when you bought this book. (Chile, I'M a different person right now than I was when I started writing). Take time to figure out what you want to do RIGHT NOW. This doesn't need to be your forever, but what is it that you LOVE to do? How can you positively impact the world around you? How can you be fulfilled?

_____

_____

_____

_____

_____

_____

_____

STEP TWO: ALIGN YOUR PURPOSE WITH WHAT YOU ARE GOOD AT.

It's easy to focus on the best (and fastest) ways to make money, so people often push their wants and needs to the back of the line. Instead of doing something they love, they do the thing that they think will make them the most money. This is often how people burn out!

I can't even tell you how many people have become my clients thinking that they would make $10 million dollars in 10 minutes only to find out that working with me means dealing with their deep soul issues. THIS. TAKES. TIME.

Rather than trying to make a lot of money really quickly, look at what you are good at and focus on aligning that with your purpose. It's not always easy to see right away, but the money WILL FOLLOW. Take the time to align your passions, skillset, and purpose. You won't need to chase money ever again.

Use this space to make a list of current passions and skills you have. Brainstorm ways you can use these to make money and then consider if these plans line up with your purpose.

Purpose Statement:

_____

_____

_____

_____

_____

_____

_____

Passion and/or Skill	How can I make money doing this?	Does it align?

Once you've figured out what you love, start brainstorming some ways you could make this into a business, or use your passions to fuel the business you are already in. What are some pain points that people have that YOUR passions and skills could rectify? If you can solve a problem, you can monetize!

Passion and/or Skill	Possible Pain Point	Am I doing this now in my business?

STEP FOUR. TAILOR YOUR OFFERING TO THE AUDIENCE YOU WANT THE MOST.

Now you want to start to think pretty specifically about the type of person you want to appeal to. Who are they? What are they into? What do they do? What gender do you want to focus on? Where do they shop? What do they believe in? Really figure out who your target is ahead of time so that you can figure out how to position your business. This will ultimately be the person you want to impact.

TARGET AVATAR NAME: _____

Age	
From	
Lives In	
Home type	
Education	
Career	
Annual Salary	
Relationship Status	
If in Relationship: Name, Age, Career?	
Biggest desire?	
Problems Achieving It	
How You Can Help	
Misc. Information About Them	

Age	
From	
Lives In	
Home type	
Education	
Career	
Annual Salary	
Relationship Status	
If in Relationship: Name, Age, Career?	
Biggest desire?	
Problems Achieving It	
How You Can Help	
Misc. Information About Them	

TARGET AVATAR NAME: _____

Age	
From	
Lives In	
Home type	
Education	
Career	
Annual Salary	
Relationship Status	
If in Relationship: Name, Age, Career?	
Biggest desire?	
Problems Achieving It	
How You Can Help	
Misc. Information About Them	

Lastly, create a solid plan. You know what you want to do and you know who you want to impact. Now, figure out how you are going to do it!

What do you need right now in order to get this ball rolling?

_____

_____

_____

_____

_____

_____

_____

Who do you need to help you get started?

_____

_____

_____

_____

_____

_____

_____

27 Me. Can You Focus on...Me?

That was cool and all, but let's get hyper-focused real quick. This teeny-tiny, itty-bitty chapter is for you to literally organize your thoughts around monetization. That's it. That's all.

What are three things you love to do?

1. _____

2. _____

3. _____

Who do you want to impact? Write down some details about the audience you want to attract and appeal to. We wrote about things like: Where do they shop? What hobbies are they into? What do they do for work?

Let's go further. What is their background? Childhood? Financial status growing up? Be as specific as you can with this one.

TARGET AVATAR 1 NAME: _____

_____

_____

_____

_____

_____

_____

_____

_____

_____

_____

_____

_____

_____

_____

_____

_____

_____

_____

_____

_____

_____

_____

_____

_____
_____
_____
_____
_____
_____
_____
_____
_____
_____
_____
_____
_____
_____
_____
_____
_____
_____
_____
_____
_____
_____

ME, CAN YOU FOCUS ON...ME?

TARGET AVATAR 3 NAME: _____

PURPOSE-DRIVEN ENTERPRISE

Now, write out some ways you could turn one of your passions into a new business, or utilize it to enhance your current business OR your position in your current company. Remember, the goal here is to do what you love to drive the coin.

Focus on what you want to do, the money will come next.

_____

_____

_____

_____

_____

_____

_____

_____

_____

_____

_____

_____

_____

_____

_____

_____

_____

_____

_____

_____

28 I'm Walking. I'm Walking. I'm Walking.

Learning about your purpose is one thing, but fully walking in it is another. When you learn to walk in your purpose, you realize that every action you take has to be aimed toward that singular goal. You start to realize how many things impact the fulfillment of your purpose. You start to create a larger audience of people around you, who are inspired by you and what you do. You start to have people who look up to you for guidance. Essentially, you gain more responsibility for the impact you have on the world.

Some key indicators that you are walking in your purpose are peace, little to no anxiety about decisions, money flowing in/no longer chasing a check, sureness, and confidence in the work you are doing.

Nixon and I started walking in our respective purpose(s) once we stopped having premarital sex. He's probably going to kill me for sharing this story, but it's 4:05 am on my final writing day so *shrugs*.

He and I had a routine whenever we were together. We spent a lot of time and money flying to each other to connect. Whether that was me flying to New York to see him, him flying to Dallas to see me, or us linking up in Chicago on business trips, we always made time for each other. Once we checked into our hotel, we would go out and grab a quick bite, then come back to do some work (remember, we're both workaholics). After a few hours of clickity-clacking on our Macbooks, we'd get dressed for our night outing where we would have dinner, go dancing, or hit the movies. Liquored up and comfortable in our sin, we'd head back to the hotel to take showers and commence to hours of passionate sex. This was our regularly scheduled routine. Neither of us felt any conviction because we knew that we were meant to be married. He was for sure my "one".

After a few years of being cozy in the 800 thread count duvet of fornication, it all came to a head. We had returned from an amazing date (I don't even remember the date now, but we always had a good time) and it was shower time. I got in the shower first as it always took me much longer to bathe. You already know. Women love to get scrubbed up and EXTRA squeaky before getting naked with their man. So I was in the shower plotting my outfit. That was the other thing. Nixon and I ALWAYS had sex like the movies - candles lit, lingerie on (then off), music playing, and wine flowing. I figured out what I was wearing as I towel dried in the master bathroom.

Nixon hopped in my shower while I lotioned down, oiled up, and got dressed. I ran downstairs to grab some bottled water from the fridge...I mean...you know...we were gonna be thirsty lol. While I was down there, I decided to use the half bath one more time just to make sure I didn't have to use the bathroom once we started. As I was sitting on the toilet, I heard God's voice SO clearly. "You have to stop doing this." I knew I was tripping. Here I was dressed in a super cute black teddy with black stockings and 6-inch heels. Nah. I was getting it in tonight. As I was washing my hands, I heard the voice again. "You can't do this anymore." Internally I asked, "How am I going to tell him?" Before I could finish the thought, God said, "I already told him." Still skeptical, I grabbed the bottled water and practically skipped up the stairs to my den of sin.

The change of atmosphere upstairs let me know that I had heard the Lord correctly downstairs. ALLLLLLL the lights were on, the candles were blown out, and the music was OFF. But the biggest indicator of trouble in paradise was Nixon's demeanor. He was sitting on the bed, fully dressed with a nervous look on his face. "Come sit down," he said softly. I felt like Adam and Eve after they had eaten the forbidden fruit and God came looking for them. I walked over to my closet, kicked off the stripper shoes, and grabbed my robe. The atmosphere had changed so much that I was literally uncomfortable being so bare.

I sat on the bed and looked sheepishly at Nixon. He said, "I have some-thing to tell you." I sat in silence as I repeated God's words over and over in my head. I couldn't believe that God was really about to shut down my intimacy with the man I was made to be with. Grabbing my hand, Nixon said, "I was in the shower and I heard God ask me if I loved you. I was like 'Of course I do.' God asked me if I wanted to marry you. I was like 'Yes. I plan on it.' And then God said 'Then you have to stop having sex with her. If you want me to bless your marriage, this stops tonight.' I didn't know how to tell you but God told me that He already talked to you…" his voice trailed off. As much as I was disappointed, I was also relieved. God knew I wasn't strong enough to stop having sex with Nixon. He had to tell Nixon to stop for us to stop.

After 25 seconds, which felt like 25 years, I told him about my own en-counter downstairs. A sigh of relief left Nixon's body and he pulled me into his arms. Our embrace was different than it had ever been. There was a love and an understanding that transcended our physical connec-tion. Even though I didn't like what God had said, I understood that I had to obey. How could I fully walk in my purpose of helping people align with God's plan for THEIR lives if I wasn't even aligned with His plan for ME?

Less than 30 days after we gave up premarital sex, both of our business-es took off. I was able to work with a couple more celebrity clients and he was able to birth an idea that God had given him nearly 20 years before.

Walking in your purpose is not easy. Obeying God means crucifying your flesh (and flesh ain't just sex). This goes back to our chat about discipline and full obedience. Not having sex has been just as hard as any fast that I've been on, but both of them have been equally pleasing in God's sight. They've also both been aids in my execution of purpose.

Here are a few things to consider when you begin this walk in your pur-pose:

The first thing is that you have to LET GO OF YOUR PLAN. God knows best, periodt! We cannot know better than our creator. This means we have to be okay with relinquishing control. Our lives are not for us. So, let go of what YOU think is best, and let God do the planning!

I could have never imagined that 7 months into a new business, I would hit 7-figures. It doesn't even fully make sense to me, but God's plan was so much better than mine. If it were up to me, I'd still be whining and complaining about my lack of direction as a fashion stylist.

Also, YOU CAN'T HOLD ON TO ONE THING. The road to purpose is not just one linear path. There are stops along the way. There are times when you'll have to hop off one train and get onto another. Times when you will have to let one thing go for something better - and that's how it's meant to be. Keep yourself God-facing, and you will continue to have what you need.

There's no way I would be traveling the country teaching people how to find their purpose and make it their paycheck if I were still stuck on my dream of being a politician. It was a dream - I woke up! Lol

You also have to learn to BE PATIENT. Patience is such a tough thing for many of us. It's hard to just wait. But it pays off when it comes to your purpose. You will receive the things that are meant for you at the time they are meant for you. Enjoy the time to have to wait. There are lessons you need to learn, and things you need to master before making it to the next step. Be patient, and focus on your purpose.

Without God slowing me down and teaching me patience, I wouldn't have the time or energy to help you with your path. I would have missed WAYYYYY too many lessons on this road and I'd honestly probably be dead. Real rap.

Also, don't be fooled. YOU CAN BE WEALTHY AND SUCCESSFUL AND NOT BE WALKING IN YOUR PURPOSE. This might sound a little spicy, but you can be super successful financially and not actually be serving your purpose. Wealth and success are not the pinnacles of purpose. There are tons of stories about multi-millionaires who are quite depressed, due to the lack of purpose in their life (look at all of the suicidal celebrities we've seen).

This is why it's important to not let money be your main motivator. Money is a tool, a means we are given to live the lifestyle we want (and to enhance the lives of others). But it cannot be the only thing that leads you. If you are on the path to success, but not able to see how this could positively impact the world around you, take time to rethink it.

And finally, TAKE ADVANTAGE OF NEW OPPORTUNITIES. The more you are walking in your purpose, the more new opportunities will pop up! Do not let fear hold you back. ***Do it scared***. Grab life by the reins, and try new things out!

Often times opportunities that we don't expect end up taking us into a whole new world where we are truly able to do what we came here to do. More opportunities are also a sign that you are on the right path. If you end up with too many and don't know which ones to take, pray about it. Talk to God, tell Him you need guidance, and He will walk you in the right direction.

Where are you right now? How can you walk in purpose? What's keeping you from giving God full ownership of your life?

_____

_____

_____

_____

_____

_____

_____

_____

29 I'm a Come Through With That Reminder

One of the main reasons we don't fully walk in purpose and maintain our position is because we don't keep our purpose in front of us. During the time I've been writing this book, I have probably been more intentional about my purpose than I've ever been. I have considered every conversation, every interaction, every phone call, every social media post...I mean EVERYTHING and evaluated whether or not it has been in alignment with my purpose.

It's so easy to be distracted by everything happening around us that it's challenging to keep your purpose alive and well. Going through the process of writing this book has shown me that walking in purpose every day requires two major things: practical advice and carrots.

If you've ever been in a class with me, then you've heard me talk about carrots. When horses race, they are often fitted with blinders to ensure they don't get distracted by other horses in the race. In addition, the jockey usually dangles a carrot directly in front of the horse to keep it going quickly on the path.

I think that every purpose-driven entrepreneur needs carrots. You need something to work towards that keeps you going when you're tired, burnt out, or distracted. So if you're wondering how I pursue purpose when I'm on empty, that's the answer - carrots.

My carrots are my unborn children. I NEVER want my kids to experience anything that I experienced. Not molestation. Not abandonment. Not rejection. Not poverty. NOTHING. So I work hard and stay in alignment with my God-given purpose so I can ensure they will have the best life possible.

My other (and even bigger) carrot? Matthew 7:21-23 KJV. "Not every one that saith unto me, Lord, Lord, shall enter into the kingdom of heaven; but he that doeth the will of my Father which is in heaven. Many will say to me in that day, Lord, Lord, have we not prophesied in thy name? and in thy name have cast out devils? and in thy name done many wonderful works? And then will I profess unto them, I never knew you: depart from me, ye that work iniquity." The SCARIEST thing in the WORLD to me is to die and meet God for Him to tell me to get out of His face because everything I did was wicked vanity. Bye!

Consider your own carrots. What are you doing all of this for? What will keep you motivated to shift your mindset?

_____

_____

_____

_____

_____

_____

_____

I told you that the other part of this was practical. So here are 5 things you can do to keep purpose in your face as you move forward:

1. Be Clear About Your Purpose

   You've got to start with clarity and positive intention. Once you have your purpose figured out, it's easy to recall. From that moment forward, all that you do has to be centered around your purpose. If you know what you need to do, you don't need to be distracted by the pull of other things. Write your purpose statement down. Memorize it. Recite it like you recite your name and date of birth.

2. Decipher Problems Keeping You From Fulfilling Your Purpose

This could be a job, a bad habit, or a person. Either way, you've got to figure it out. Sometimes we don't realize we could be the one holding ourselves back from fulfilling our purpose. Whatever it is, eliminate it immediately. It's not always an easy, or quick process, but once it's done, it's DONE! You will start to see the path opening up pretty quickly once you are on it.

3. Decide Where You Want to Go Next

So you've figured out what your purpose is, but you have no real idea about what you want to do next. You're good at a lot of things, but as your purpose evolves you'll start wanting to do new things. And that's okay! Whatever you decide, know that you don't have to be stuck in one place forever. If you can't figure out the first step, ask God. Tell Him you don't know what you need, or where to go. Let Him guide you.

When you get your answer, be sure about it and go there immediately. Remember, delayed obedience is disobedience.

4. Make Your Purpose a Part of Your Everyday Life

Again, everything you do has to be geared towards your purpose. That means you'll have to start forming new habits to keep you on the path to purpose. Connect with your creator every day. Consult with Him. Do new things every day. Do things that make you feel good, and things that positively impact the people in your life and the world around you.

5. Find Time for Stillness

Find some time in your day or at least week where you can just be still. You can't hear God if you are constantly distracted by noise. You can't focus on yourself and your inner thoughts if you are constantly focusing on others. Take some time to just stop, don't do anything, and be still. This will help hone your focus on your purpose.

Let's do one more exercise for the road. Take a moment to get still and consider your best life. The focus of this activity is to give you clarity about your purpose, and how to prioritize it. We're going to be using the phrase "My life is ideal when I'm _____." Think of things that make you feel good, and fulfilled.

1. My life is ideal when I'm _____

2. My life is ideal when I'm _____

3. My life is ideal when I'm _____

4. My life is ideal when I'm _____

5. My life is ideal when I'm _____

6. My life is ideal when I'm _____

7. My life is ideal when I'm _____

8. My life is ideal when I'm _____

9. My life is ideal when I'm _____

10. My life is ideal when I'm _____

Now, identify the top 5 choices. To do this, you'll compare statements #1 and #2 to identify which is most important. Eliminate the least important one. Continue with each statement until you only have 5 remaining.

1. _____

2. _____

3. _____

4. _____

5. _____

Use these 5 statements as a basis for purpose. You know that these 5 things make you feel the most fulfilled. If you know when your life is most ideal, everything you do should be based on those statements.

Assume that the world is perfect. What does it look like? What does it feel like? How are people interacting? Who are you? Write this statement out in the present tense as if it's happening right now.

_____

_____

_____

_____

_____

_____

_____

_____

_____

_____

_____

_____

_____

30 The ~~Emancipation~~ Evolution of ~~Mimi~~ Purpose

I can't believe our time together is over. I mean…"We Belong Together" lol. Get it? Mariah Carey title with a referen- never mind.

You've done so much work over the last [insert however long it took you to get to the end]. I'm proud of you frfr. I want you to use this book as a guide for your LIFE. When you feel stuck or unsure, come back here and dig in. Every time you open this book, I pray that you gain new insight and revelation. If you feel stuck or you want to share a testimonial on how this book changed your life, shoot me a DM at instagram.com/iamkendrayhill or an email at heyhey@kendrascalemybusiness.com. I will read it and respond. Promise.

But we aren't actually done yet. One of my biggest philosophies around purpose hasn't fully been shared yet. We still got some time together!

One of the main questions I get concerning purpose is whether or not your purpose changes over time. The short answer is NO. Your purpose is your purpose is your purpose, okay?! But what DOES happen is that the manifestation of your purpose evolves over time.

The evolution of purpose is not a drastic change. If you find that your purpose today is totally different than it was in the past, you probably weren't aligned with your purpose in the first place, or you just didn't truly know what it was. As your purpose evolves, it becomes sharp and more focused, but it stays natural. It's a sign that we are actually growing. This mostly happens when our focus shifts from ourselves to the outside world (as we discussed in earlier chapters, purpose is not about us, but our impact on the world around us).

Before you've even started to search for your purpose, you're being guided to it. You're getting hints, and nudges in small ways towards your overall goal. For most people, it's delivered as a seed that grows as we grow. We aren't always ready for the end result - the full bloom of that seed. We have to plant it, water it, let the sunshine hit it. Storms have to come to test the strength of its stem. Strong winds make it stronger, and more adaptable. In different seasons its petals might fall off, but in their place grows something stronger, more vibrant, more sure. That is the evolution of purpose.

Let's say, for example, your purpose in life is to help people heal through their past and connect/strengthen their spiritual selves. For some people that might mean they take on roles like a life coach, therapist, or some role in the mental health sector. But that doesn't mean that that's the only way to fulfill your purpose. This "person" most likely didn't head straight to that conclusion. There is usually an evolution that takes place earlier on to put them in that position.

During one season, God might put certain people in your path to guide you there. Let's say you are working a part-time job at the mall. Then one day a customer comes up to you and starts pouring into you. Maybe this is someone you started building a connection with over a few visits to your store, or maybe it's someone who just walked in and needed to vent. You listen, maybe share some advice, and that person walks away with a lighter heart and head. In turn, YOU walk away feeling just as light and more accomplished from that conversation than you did all day at work. You might feel your purpose is to listen to people - to HEAR people. But that's just a start. As you grow, your purpose becomes focused and clear. That might eventually take you down the path to mental health work, or coaching. Later on in life, your purpose could manifest as pastoring a church. THAT is an example of purpose evolving. That might have been one of the more memorable first tastes of your purpose. You aren't a therapist or a coach, but it doesn't matter. In this season, you're exactly where you're meant to be.

It's also important to note that purpose really shows itself during challenging or transitional times. Whether that's some personal crisis, loss of a person, a big move, or some type of big change in our lives. We end up in scenarios that are so far out of our comfort zone, which forces us to not only ask new questions but reformulate questions we already had.

The real secret to purpose is to keep updating your purpose iOS. What do I mean? We get frustrated when we find ourselves stagnant and unsure. We also get kinda pissy when we see other people "getting ahead" or operating in their purpose when we feel like we should be ahead of them. Well…if you're operating old software, it's no wonder others are getting ahead, babe. Those people updated to the new purpose iOs (internal operating system).

Every time God wants to use you in a new way to fulfill purpose (i.e. going from a coach to a pastor or an assistant to an artist), you have to upgrade your system. And you already know the only way to upgrade your software - you gotta check those system preferences in prayer. Periodt. You can only update by spending time with God and checking your notifications.

You know how on your smartphone you get that notification that says that a software update is available? And you know how you keep pressing "later" so you don't have to deal with it? Well after months of ignoring it, what happens? You go to sleep and you wake up to a phone that has a brand new update. You were forced to accept the new software. Don't put God in a situation where He has to force you to take the update.

Listen. I hope that all of this has been helpful. Again, use this book as a guide. Staying on track with your purpose is a continuous journey. You never actually "arrive"- you just keep updating. When you feel lost lost, go back to your Golden Spoon and start there. Continue to stay connected to your creator and check for new updates along the way.

Made in the USA
Las Vegas, NV
08 May 2023

71779101R00136